T0143542

Elements of Multimedia

Elements of Multimedia

Sreeparna Banerjee

CRC Press is an imprint of the
Taylor & Francis Group, an **informa** business
A CHAPMAN & HALL BOOK

CRC Press
Taylor & Francis Group
52 Vanderbilt Avenue,
New York, NY 10017

Printed on acid-free paper

International Standard Book Number-13: 978-1-138-36037-2 (Hardback)

Library of Congress Cataloging-in-Publication Data

Names: Banerjee, Sreeparna, author.
Title: Elements of multimedia / Sreeparna Banerjee.
Description: Boca Raton : Taylor & Francis, a CRC title, part of the Taylor & Francis imprint, a member of the Taylor & Francis Group, the academic division of T&F Informa, plc, 2019. | Includes bibliographical references and index.
Identifiers: LCCN 2019010551 | ISBN 9781138360372 (hardback : acid-free paper) | ISBN 9780429433207 (ebook)
Subjects: LCSH: Multimedia systems.
Classification: LCC QA76.575 .B356 2019 | DDC 006.7--dc23
LC record available at https://lccn.loc.gov/2019010551

Visit the Taylor & Francis Web site at
http://www.taylorandfrancis.com

and the CRC Press Web site at
http://www.crcpress.com

To the persons who shaped my life during the formative years:

My parents

My sister

and

My affectionate maternal grandparents

Contents

List of Figures

List of Tables

Preface

Elements of Multimedia is an outgrowth of lectures delivered for a multimedia technology course for B.Tech and M.Tech in information technology and computer science. Hence, many resources, including the World Wide Web, have been used in their preparation. Some examples and images have been taken from the Internet. However, the scope of the book covers a much wider field and encompasses other disciplines such as computer applications, multimedia and graphics, and computer science, to name a few.

The objective of the book is to cover the diverse range of multimedia topics in one comprehensive volume. Questions and case studies are provided wherever appropriate to instill an interest in the subject and to activate a desire to explore the subject at greater depth.

With these objectives in mind, the book sets out to present the various aspects of multimedia. The field covers computer science, electrical engineering, physics, and communication technologies on one hand, and management, art, and creativity on the other. Thus, the field includes studies in both science-based subjects as well as subjects related to art and design. However, computers and modern-day smartphones and tablets, with various adaptations, form the common platform to integrate these diverse fields. This is where multimedia comes in.

Elements of Multimedia begins, in Chapter 1, with an overview of multimedia systems, their platforms, various adaptations that make the computer a multimedia platform, and also some important applications. This is followed by chapters on various elements of multimedia, for example, text, audio, image, graphics, animation, and video, in Chapters 2 through 6. These chapters provide technical discourses that give a clear understanding of these topics. Some of these elements, for example, audio and video, are streaming data and therefore consume a lot of memory. Thus, compression of data is an important consideration, and this topic is treated in Chapter 7. As multimedia applications are in the areas of e-commerce, industry, and entertainment, the creation of multimedia content and its presentation constitute the subject matter of Chapter 8. Storage aspects, both in hardware as well as databases, and retrieval of multimedia content are presented in Chapter 9. Chapter 10, the final chapter, deals with communication and networking issues.

The objectives of each chapter are presented at the beginning of each chapter. Reviews are presented at the end of each chapter. For the benefit of students' preparation and exploring, review questions and multiple-choice questions are also provided.

To use the book effectively in its entirety, a mathematics course at the high school level is recommended. However, in the absence of this background, some sections of Chapters 3 and 7 may be omitted without much loss of information. Learning resources such as solutions to problems will be provided when possible.

Author

Sreeparna Banerjee, formerly Head of the Departments of Natural Science and Industrial Engineering and Management, at Maulana Abul Kalam Azad University of Technology (formerly West Bengal University of Technology), West Bengal, Kolkata, completed her PhD in Physics at the University of Virginia in the United States. Subsequently, she has taught physics and information technology subjects, including multimedia technology and applications, in India and abroad. *Elements of Multimedia* is an outgrowth of the lectures on multimedia. She has conducted research in various areas such as artificial intelligence (AI), machine learning, pattern recognition, and computer vision applications in astrophysics, meteorology, and biomedical image processing, in addition to physics. Her research has resulted in more than 80 publications in peer-reviewed national and international journals, edited books, and conference proceedings.

1

Multimedia Systems

1.1 Introduction

Multimedia has become a buzzword [1–7] for computer and mobile environments due to their myriad uses. However, the multimedia experience in the virtual world of a computer or mobile phone system is an attempt to mimic real-life experiences by activating the senses of humans, namely, sight, hearing, and touch. Multimedia uses different elements such as audio, images, graphics, and animation. Thus, multimedia creates an audiovisual environment either on the desktop or on the smartphone screen, as well as over local and global environments. Not only does multimedia store different media types as digital data but it also produces highly structured databases that can be interactively accessed and manipulated by users.

Multimedia has many uses in industry, entertainment, education, and government, to name a few. Business applications include advertising, product demos, marketing, training, networked communications, catalogs, and voicemail.

In education, multimedia enhances the teaching-learning process by simulating information and use of audiovisual aids. At home, TV programs can provide instructions on cooking, gardening, and interior design. Public places like airports, rail stations, and shopping malls also utilize multimedia. Virtual reality is a multimedia extension that uses animation, sound, and images.

With the evolution of multimedia to digital media and new media, the craving for multimedia has also increased. Web 1.0 is being superseded by Web 2.0, which marks the transition from the passive use of web content to interactive use. This in turn has paved the way for social networking, a very popular activity today for connecting with people, for either business or social purposes. Even text has its uses in communication: text messages bear testimony to this fact. Hence, an understanding of multimedia in the virtual world is important for applications in the real world.

This chapter gives an overview of multimedia, its uses, how personal computers (PCs) and smartphones can be made to function as multimedia platforms, multimedia objects, and a description of the components of a multimedia workstation.

1.1.1 What Is Multimedia?

Multimedia [1–6] is a computer platform, communications network, or a software tool that incorporates the interactive use of at least one of the following types of information: audio, image, animation, video, text, and graphics. The elements of a multimedia system include:

- Processor: for example, computer/workstation enhanced to handle audio or video
- Variety of methods for user interaction: for example, keyboard, mouse, joystick, or touchscreen
- Screen: to display high-quality still images and moving video
- Microphone: way to play back prerecorded source material, usually from some form of optical disc, for example, a compact disc

Unlike mass media or old media, examples of which include newspaper and television, multimedia is interactive and supported on a digital platform, where one can edit the multimedia content. In today's context, multimedia has evolved as digital media or new media [8].

Mobile technology also provides platforms for multimedia mobile applications (apps) that are used for different applications. An application programming interface (API) allows different software applications to communicate with each other.

1.1.1.1 New Media

Compared to old media or mass media like radio, television, and printed newspapers, new media [8] refers to media that is digital and is native to computers. Essentially, new media is interactive and provides two-way communication and involves computations. Examples of new media are computers, virtual worlds, single media, website games, human-computer interfacing, online encyclopedias like Wikipedia, interactive computer installation, and computer animation. Blogs, social media, digital games, virtual reality, and online newspapers constitute forms of new media.

1.1.1.2 Digital Media

Digital media [8] is the successor of multimedia. It also uses computer technology to combine various forms of media. It is electronic media that works using digital codes as opposed to analog signals/continuous signals. Using digital signals, it creates digital audio, digital video, and other digital content.

Digital media finds use in the creation of presentations, tutorials, simulations, games, and web pages, to name a few. The five major elements of digital media are audio, video, graphics, animation, and web design. Examples of digital media include apps on smartphones, video game console, and medical imaging devices like ultrasonographs.

Digital media requires a diverse set of skills like artistic skills, technical skills, and analytical and product coordination skills. Thus, digital media is useful for entertainment industries, e-commerce, health, education, marketing and advertising, defense and government, sports, television broadcasting, and publishing.

1.1.2 Categories of Multimedia

Multimedia can be categorized as linear or nonlinear. Linear multimedia progresses sequentially, without navigation control just like mass media. Nonlinear multimedia allows user interaction and navigation control. Nonlinear multimedia is also known as hypermedia content.

Multimedia presentations can be live or recorded. The live category allows interaction with the presenter/performer, while the recorded category only permits interaction via navigation system.

Based on the type of object used, a multimedia element can also be classified as nontemporal (e.g., image, text) or static data or temporal (audio, video) for streaming data. Multimedia consists of at least one static and one temporal element.

1.2 Multimedia Platforms

The IBM PC compatible machine is not a natural multimedia platform. Audio and video adapters, as well as extensions to the operating system, are required. Essential developments in PC architecture that have improved support for multimedia are:

- *Audio and video adapters*: Earlier versions used boards to digitize images as well as boards to capture, digitize, compress, decompress, and play back motion video.
- *Bus architecture*: *Data bus* is an internal communication line that carries data from one part of the computer to another. The amount of information that a computer can carry is its bandwidth, measured by its frequency range (MHz or Kb/s). Existing buses carry small packets of data, but audio and video require transmission of continuous data streams. In order to support multimedia applications, requirements for any new data bus must include:
    - Increased speed
    - Standardization to encourage an active market for third-party peripherals at low cost
    - Compatibility with existing market for adapter boards

To transmit multimedia information over a network, the separate voice, video, and data streams must be first merged (multiplexed) into a single stream in the computer. This stream is then de-multiplexed by the computer that receives it. Implementation of multiplexing is a software (S/W) function requiring additional processing and possible extensions. To avoid "jerky" playback and to ensure smooth audio and video, the data paths from audio and video should be separate from computational data paths.

Most recent multimedia platform (e.g., manila PCs) motherboards come with sound chips and graphics co-processors, and the use of industry standard architecture (ISA) bus is also obviated. Separate graphics cards are used only for high-end purposes.

1.3 Multimedia Applications

Multimedia applications are used in diverse areas, including information, entertainment, communication, education, and private and public sectors. Application types can be classified as local or distributed. Basic multimedia services include information retrieval, information recording and editing, and interpersonal communication. The modes can be individual and bulk communication as well as synchronous and asynchronous communication. Some examples of multimedia applications, including applications at business and work as well as education and entertainment, are described below.

1.3.1 Video on Demand (VOD)

Video on demand (VOD) is used for the storage, transmission, and display of archived video files in a networked environment. The most popular use is watching movies provided by the cable service provider. VOD includes audio and rich media on demand. Examples of VOD services include YouTube, MSN video, Google video, and content distribution services (CDNs). VOD consumes a large amount of computer storage and network capacity.

A VOD system either "streams" content, allowing real-time viewing, or "downloads" it in its entirety in a set-top box before viewing starts. This is termed "store and forward." VOD streams content through a set-top box to enable real-time viewing or downloads the content to a digital video recorder (also known as a personal video recorder) or a portable media player for later viewing. VOD faces stiff competition from Netflix, Hulu, and so on.

1.3.1.1 Video Streaming

YouTube is a video-sharing website that allows users to upload, view, share and rate user- and corporate-generated content. Users can add content to favorites, report and comment on videos, and subscribe to other users.

Hulu is a video-streaming service that offers premium video content from TV shows as well as feature films. A small monthly subscription entitles users to gain access to everything on Hulu. Unlimited streaming is possible. Unlike user-generated video sites like YouTube, Hulu offers TV shows and partnerships with various studios, such as MGM, Warner Brothers, and Sony Pictures. TV shows are available through a joint venture with NBC Universal, Fox Entertainment, and ABC Inc.

Netflix is another video-streaming service, started in 1977, that partnered with LG to introduce the first Blu-ray Disc player to Internet for streaming purposes. This is also a subscription-based service and is more expensive than Hulu. In Netflix, content can be accessed through smart TVs, Blu-ray Disc players, media streamers, game consoles, smartphones, and tablets. Its joint ventures for TV shows are with ABC, CBS, Fox, NBC, WB, and AMC, to name a few. It has hidden genre and original categories as well. There are also software programs for download and provisions for three-dimensional (3D) content selection.

1.3.2 Multimedia Mail

Multimedia mail incorporates text, audio, video, and so on, in mail document. Multimedia Internet Mail Extension (MIME) is an internet standard that extends the email format to support both text (in ASCII as well as other character sets) and nontext attachments, message bodies with multiple parts, and even headers in non-ASCII character sets. It consists of several parts, and each part might have different types: text, audio, video, graphics, image, and so on. A typical MIME message must include data in multiple message parts, definition of content types of individual parts, and boundaries between the parts.

Snapchat is a multimedia messaging app used globally. It was developed by students at Stanford University. Pictures and messages are available for messaging for a short time.

1.3.3 Multimedia Conferencing

Multimedia based conferencing and collaboration is used in integrated services digital network (ISDN) and local area network (LAN)/Internet-based telephony and conferencing. It is also used for telenetworking like in computer-supported cooperative work (CSCW), a design-oriented work that brings together academicians of various disciplines. All persons can see the same information, as in what you see is what I see (WYSWIS). Another use is in application sharing.

Video conferencing, also known as video teleconferencing, is a set of interactive telecommunication technologies that allows two or more locations to interact via two-way video and audio transmissions simultaneously. It is also called visual collaboration and is a groupware.

Today, mobile operating systems like Android, iOS for Apple, Symbian for Nokia, and Blackberry OS for RIM are all operating systems designed to enable mobile conferencing using multimedia elements on smartphones and tablets. Android has a touchscreen interface as well as other features and apps that render it as a smartphone.

Android is a mobile operating system (OS) based on the Linux kernel that has been developed by Google.

1.3.4 Multicast Backbone

Multicast Backbone (Mbone) is operated by public domain software. The services include: (1) transfer of multimedia data over the Internet and (2) providing a virtual network based on the Internet.

1.3.5 Multimedia Kiosks

A multimedia kiosk is a physical structure including a multimedia-based computer that displays information for people walking by. In addition, users can interact by using touchscreens and sound and motion videos. These kiosks allow stand-up or walk-on services.

1.3.6 Interactive Television (iTV)

Interactive television (iTV) allows a return path; that is, information can flow from the broadcaster to the viewer as well as from the viewer to the broadcaster. Each TV set is offered a choice of content. Uses include:

1. T-commerce, to order things without using a phone
2. The ability to pause live TV shows and click on "find out more" in advertisements
3. Click stream analysis; that is, every click of the viewer goes into a database to create a profile of the viewer for later interaction

1.3.6.1 HDTV, 4K, and 8K

High-definition TV (HDTV) [9] provides substantially higher resolution than a standard definition TV (SDTV). HDTV use once used analog technology, but now transmission occurs digitally using video compression.

1. HD ready: 720p: has a resolution of 1280 × 720p = 923600 pixels (approximately 0.92 MP per frame)
2. Full HD: 1080i: 1920 × 1080i = 1036800i pixels per field or 2073600 pixels per frame (approximately 2.07 MP)
3. Full HD: 1080p = 2073600p (approximately 2.07MP)

In the list above, p stands for "progressive" and i stand for "interlaced." At 2 MP per frame, the HDTV resolution is five times that of SDTV.

Ultra-high definition (UHD) has very high resolutions and has two categories: 8K UHD has a resolution of 7680 × 4320, or 33.2 MP; 4K UHD has a resolution of 3840 × 2160 for HD and 4096 × 2160 for a digital camera.

1.3.6.2 Modern TV

Modern TVs [10] do not use cathode ray tubes (CRTs).

Plasma TVs use plasma displays, which include small cells containing electrically charged (ionized) gases or plasmas. The screen size of plasma TVs is typically between 42″ and 65″. They have excellent viewing angle, very good picture contrast, excellent video motion and color gamut, and good power consumption.

Liquid crystal display (LCD) TVs have a fluorescent (or cold cathode fluorescent lamp [CCLF]) backlight. Light emitting diode (LEDs) can be placed either behind the TV screen or around its edges. LED TVs have the same LCD screen; hence, these TVs are often termed as LED-LCD TVs. LED TVs are more energy efficient and a lot smaller than a CCFL enabling a thinner TV screen. The contrast and colors are also better.

Both LED and LCD TVs have screen sizes from 19″ to 84″. Other qualities are comparable to plasma TVs. The power consumption is excellent and much better than plasma TVs. Plasma TVs generate more heat and are thicker and heavier than the LCD and LED TVs; thus, plasma TVs are not much used today.

1.3.7 Educational Applications

Due to the integration of different media, e-learning has a better impact than conventional learning. Some examples where such learning is proving to be useful are:

CyberMath

Scientific American

Discovery Online

National Geographic

1.3.8 Multimedia Archives and Digital Libraries

Multimedia archives link to large repositories of sound, pictures, and animation files available on the Internet. Digital libraries are collections stored in digital format and are accessible by computer.

1.3.9 Media Editors

Media editors are software packages used to create multimedia presentations and packages. Some examples are:

Authorware by Adobe Systems
Director by Adobe systems
Flash by Adobe systems
Producer by Microsoft

1.3.10 Web 2.0 Technology

Web 2.0 [11] embodies the changing trends in the functionality of the World Wide Web (WWW) as we know it, that is, Web 1.0. Web 2.0 is the evolution of Web use from passive use of content to interactive use by allowing participation, creation of content, and content sharing. Users can thus coauthor data in Web 2.0 and exercise control over it. The capabilities of Web 2.0 include the following:

- Providing information search using keywords
- Allowing authoring capabilities by creating and updating content created by other users
- Using single word tags to categorize content
- Providing extensions for automation of pattern matching
- Use of real-time syndication (RSS) signals to update users about changes in content

Some popular Web 2.0 tools and their functionality are listed below:

1. Blogs: A blog (or Weblog) is a personal journal on the Web. It constitutes a fluid medium that provides a platform for reading, writing, and commenting. The blogger writes a blog (or entry, post, or posting) addressed to the blogosphere comprising a community of bloggers. Readers can post their comments on it. Unlike journalism, which attempts to be objective in nature, blogging is subjective and conveys the opinions of the individuals creating or commenting on the blog. A permalink is a permanent identifier for a specific Weblog post. A list of blogs and bloggers included on the site of the blog appear in a blogroll.
2. Podcasting: Podcasting is the distribution of multimedia files like audio and video files over the Internet for playback on mobile devices and PCs. *Pod* is the mobile playback device (e.g., iPod, laptop, or PC), and *casting* is the process of broadcasting. Podcasts are shared or syndicated in the RSS format.

3. Social networking: Social networking constitutes a virtual community on a website to share information or just interact with each other. Members create their profile page with personal information and can communicate with other members of their choice via multimedia elements like text, voice, chat, instant messaging, video conferencing, and blogs. Some popular social networking websites are Facebook and LinkedIn.
4. Wiki: A wiki is a Web page or collection of Web pages that can be expanded or modified by users. Thus, documents or content can be written collaboratively or iteratively in a simple mark-up language using a Web browser. The online encyclopedia Wikipedia is the most popular example.
5. Electronic portfolios: Electronic portfolios (or e-portfolios or Webfolios) are digital versions of traditional portfolios. They provide a digital resource of a wide range of information and content for education, personal information presentations, papers, and other work. Uses in education include coursework where assignments and projects as well as instructor comments are incorporated. Personal e-portfolios include personal information, education and employment history, goals, and activities, to name a few.
6. Micro-blogging: Micro-blogging is also known as mobile social networking or themed instant messaging. It enables users to write brief messages up to 200 characters and publish them via Web-browser-based services, email, or mobile phones. Twitter is the most popular micro-blogging service.
7. Social bookmarking: Social bookmarking is a way to store, organize, search, manage, and share collections of websites using metadata tags or keywords that can be shared across the Internet.

1.3.11 Social Media

Social networking on social media [12] uses the Internet to connect users with their friends, family members, and acquaintances. The most popular social media platforms are Facebook, Twitter, LinkedIn, and Instagram.

"Friends" in Facebook or "followers" in Twitter can be connected to each other to share information, photos, and video on these websites, which also allow the organization of events, chats, and online game playing.

When signing up with a social media website, a profile page can be created after email ID verification. The information on this profile depends on the user, who can provide a picture and other personal information as desired.

Such social media websites have a variety of privacy settings that can be adjusted by the user, who has control over who can access this profile page. The link called "Settings" provides the user with a list of adjustments.

On social media, "friends" can be made by the social media user by sending a "friend request." Once the request accepted, the user is able to interact with the "friend."

1.3.12 Mobile Media

Multimedia content like audio, images, and video can be captured and shared through mobile media [13].

1.4 Multimedia Building Blocks

The multimedia object element supports different media types like text, images, graphics, audio, and video. These are described briefly below.

1.4.1 Text

The simplest form of multimedia is text. It has been used since the advent of computers for storing information in traditional files. Text is composed of strings of characters entered at a keyboard to form words, sentences, paragraphs. and even whole articles. These characters could be alphanumeric characters as well as punctuation marks. They can include both ASCII characters as well as control characters. Text is used to communicate ideas in documents. Text has uses in writing documents on computers as well as for interactions through mobile phones and smartphones.

1.4.1.1 Text Messaging

WhatsApp is a messaging app. By using this app, users can chat, send text, and share media, including voice messages and video, with individuals and groups. Data to send messages is sent using iMessage or black berry messenger (BBM) so that it does not consume the monthly text allotment. Essentially, WhatsApp is a cross-platform, an instant messaging app that allows the use of the iPhone, Blackberry, Android, Windows phone, and Nokia smartphone. With WhatsApp, one can make audio as well as video calls.

Short messaging service (SMS) was defined in the 1985 global system for mobile communication (GSM) standards. Short messages are sent over cellular networks. Messages of up to 160 characters can be sent at a time. The maximum size depends on the carriers, but 300 kB is the largest size permitted.

In multimedia messaging service (MMS), audio and video, in addition to text, can be sent over cellular networks, but there is no size limit. WhatsApp and iMessage are over-the-top (OTT), which uses internet protocol (IP). No cellular connection is required, but an Internet connection through Wi-Fi or mobile Internet is required. Furthermore, OTT apps need to be downloaded. However, OTT apps are free.

SMS is supported on all mobile phones, and MMS is supported on most smartphones, so both are paid services through the cellular connection service provider. OTT apps have no file limit and are also free, so they are often preferred over MMS.

1.4.1.2 Communicating Emotions via Text

Text is used to communicate emotions through the use of emoticons (Figure 1.1) and emojis (Figure 1.2) [14]. An emoticon is a pictorial representation of a facial expression using characters that are present on a computer keyboard. These characters can be punctuation marks, numbers, and letters

FIGURE 1.1
Social media concept. (Created by Rawpixel.com-Freepik.com.)

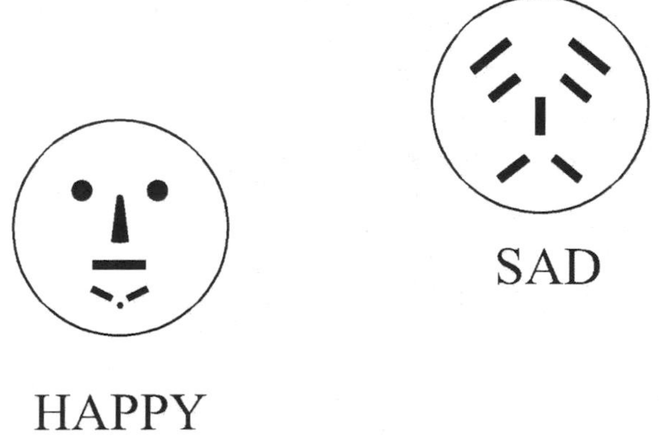

FIGURE 1.2
Examples of emoticons.

FIGURE 1.3
An emoji.

that portray a person's feelings or moods. Emoticons and emojis are time-saving method. An emoji is a more recent invention. Emojis are pictographs of faces, objects, and symbols (Figure 1.3).

1.4.2 Graphics

Computer-generated images are referred to as computer graphics or graphics. They are composed of all kinds of objects: **visual**, for example, lines, arcs, curves, and so on, as well as hand-drawn (**free-form**) objects. Attributes of objects include shape, size, and so on Closed objects can be filled with color to create solid objects; this process is known as rendering. The gallery of images that come with a graphics package is referred to as **clip art**. The generated image is displayed on the screen. The computer's display screen is made up of a two-dimensional (2D) matrix of individual picture elements called **pixels**, each of which can have a range of colors associated with it. For example, video graphics array (**VGA**) consists of 640 horizontal pixels by 480 vertical pixels with 8 bits per pixel, which allows each pixel to have 256 colors.

VGA is an analog signal interface and has been replaced by digital interfaces like HDMI, DVI, and DisplayPort, depending on the applications for which they are used.

1.4.3 Images

Images are visual representations of real-life scenes captured by a sensor like a camera. Images can be 2D (e.g., a photograph) or 3D (e.g., a statue or hologram).

When scanners are used for digitizing continuous monochromatic images (e.g., a printed picture or scene) more than a single bit is used to digitize each picture element to produce an image. For example, black and white pictures (**bitonic images)** requires two bits per pixel. A gray-level image is generated typically by using 8 bits per pixel or picture element (pel), to 256 gray levels. Color images are formed from combinations of the three primary colors of red, green, and blue. For each of these three colors, 8 bits per pixel are used, adding up to 24 bits per pixel. Computer screens display color images using three electron guns, each of which has a primary color. The resulting image is due to color mixing from the three channels. Picture tubes in TVs operate on the principle of raster scan, where raster is a finely focused electron beam. A complete scan (frame) comprises several discrete horizontal lines (N) starting at top left and ending at bottom right. To display continuous images, it is necessary to continuously refresh the screen (the rate at which this is done is called the frame refresh rate). Some other properties of multimedia images are:

- Pixel depth: number of bits per pixel determines the range of different colors that can be produced, for example, 12 bits with 4 bits/primary color yields 4096 different colors.
- Aspect ratio: the ratio of the screen width to the screen height.
- Image sensor: the image sensor is usually a solid-state device known as a charge-coupled device (**CCD**) that is used to capture images.

1.4.4 Audio

Audio is sound with a frequency range that is typically available to humans. Audio waves (or signals) are longitudinal mechanical waves produced by compression and rarefaction of the material medium of propagation. There are three types of audio signal:

- Speech (bandwidth: 50 Hz–10 KHz) signals (e.g., telephony/video telephony)
- Music-quality signals (15 Hz–20 kHz) (e.g., CD on demand and broadcast television)
- Sound (2 Hz–20 kHz)

Audio signals can be produced naturally with a microphone (analog signal) or with a synthesizer (digital) format. Musical signals use musical instrument digital interface (**MIDI**), while speech signals can be digitized using pulse code modification (**PCM**).

1.4.5 Video

Video is an electronic technology that involves capturing, recording, storing, processing, transmitting, and reconstructing a sequence of still images that record scenes in motion. The minimum refresh rate of the series of images (or frames) should be around 50/sec to avoid flicker, but for a smooth refresh rate, 25 times/sec is enough. To minimize the amount of transmission bandwidth required to broadcast a TV signal, this property transmits images and pictures associated with each frame by splitting the frame into two halves, each being known as a field (the first comprises odd scan lines and the second comprises even scan lines). This technique is known as interleaved scanning. For color signals, three main properties of the light signal are used, namely, the brightness (luminance), which is the amount of energy that stimulates the eye, with black as the minimum and white as the maximum; hue (actual color of the source); and saturation (strength/vividness of the color). Hue and saturation are referred to as chrominance characteristics.

1.4.6 Simulation and Morphing

Simulation refers to the emulation of physical events on a computer screen, with possible integration of audio, video, animation, and, of course, graphics. Morphing refers to translation, rotation, scaling, and shearing of an image to change the shape of an image, for example, a cat can be "morphed" to produce a dog. Morphing comprises two steps:

- Warping of the host image
- Dissolving the warped image into the target image

1.4.7 Animation

Animation is an illusion of movement created by sequentially playing still image frames at the rate of 15–20 frames/sec. Methods of animation are:

- Toggling between image frames: changing images at display times.
- Rotating through several image frames.
- Delta frame animation: After display of the initial image frame, successive frames are based on what has changed. Changes are called delta. One advantage of this technique is that less memory space is required.
- Palette animation: Image frames are either drawn or bit-blited to the screen. Palette animation involves drawing objects and manipulating palette colors or just manipulating these colors, for example, a wheel with different colors.

- Motion graphics [15] are pieces of digital footage or animation that create the illusion of motion. In multimedia projects, audio is also incorporated with animation.
- Visual effects (VFX) refer to the process of creating imagery and manipulating it outside the context of the actual filmmaking process. Live action footage is the special effect of integrating live action with the generated imagery, referred to as digital effects, to give it a realistic appearance. These effects can be created using computer-generated imagery and easy-to-use animation tools.
- Character animation involves bringing animated characters to life. It appears as if the character animator is a film or stage actor with a pencil. A lifelike appearance of the character is imbued to give the illusion of thought, emotion, and personality. Creature animation involves making animals and creatures photorealistic.

1.4.8 Hypertext and Hypermedia

For typical text, for example, a book, one must read from the first page or chapter to the next page or chapter, and so on, in a sequential fashion. However, for hypertext, one can jump or navigate from one portion of the text to another portion with the help of links. The addition of other media types, such as audio, video, and so on, to hypertext is referred to as hypermedia. Hypertext and hypermedia are essential components of a multimedia system.

More detailed descriptions will be covered in the ensuing chapters.

1.5 Multimedia Systems

A typical multimedia system consists of five components:

1. Connecting devices
2. Input devices
3. Output devices
4. Storage devices
5. Communicating devices

1.5.1 Connecting Devices

The most popularly used connecting devices are:

1. Small computer system interface (SCSI) is a set of standards for physically connecting and transferring data between computers and peripherals.

2. The media control interface (MCI) typically consists of four parts: (i) AVI video, (ii) CD audio, (iii) sequencer, and (iv) waveaudio, with each of these devices playing certain types of files.
3. The integrated drive electronics (IDE) interface is a standard way for storage devices to connect to a computer.
4. These first three devices have become obsolete and currently the USB is used.
5. The universal serial bus (USB) is a serial bus standard for interface devices.

1.5.1.1 Universal Serial Bus (USB)

The USB [16,17] is a common serial interface that enables the communication between external peripheral devices like hard disc and flash drives, digital cameras, mice, keyboards, printers, scanners, and media devices with a host controller like a PC or a laptop. Due to its wide range of applications, the USB has replaced several interfaces like the parallel and serial ports.

The salient features of USB include plug-and-play enhancement as well as the ability to perform hot swapping. Using plug and play, the OS can spontaneously configure and discover a new peripheral device without the necessity of restarting the computer. Hot swapping allows the removal and replacement of a new peripheral without rebooting.

Most USB connectors come in two types. Type A is the USB 2.0 standard. The type A interface has a flat rectangular interface that inserts into a hub or a USB host that supplies power as well as transmits data. Common examples of type A USB devices arc keyboards and mice.

A type B USB connector is square shaped, has slanted corners, and is connected to an upstream port that uses a removable cable, as for a printer. Like the type A connector, the type B connector also supplies power and transmits data. However, some type B connectors are only used for power connection and do not have data connection. The type C connector for USB 3.0 is a 24-pin connector that has a twofold rotational symmetric connector.

USB 3.0 is the third major revision by USB-IF, renamed USB 3.1 Gen. No other technical improvement has resulted in a tenfold increase in performance and better power management. This performance increase is due to USB Gen 3.1 Gen 1 technology, which enables multiple streams of data transfer and boosts the peak signaling band width from 480 Mbps (for USB 2.0) to 5 Gbps. Actual transfer speeds depend on controller and not AND (NAND) configurations.

Originally co-invented by Ajay Bhatt at Intel, the development of USB was later taken up by several companies in 1994, namely, Compaq, Microsoft, IBM, Digital Equipment Corporation, Nortel, and NEC corporation, with the objective of facilitating the connection of peripheral devices to a PC without the use of many connectors. Factors taken into consideration in developing USB included the creation of larger bandwidths and streamlining of software configurations.

The standard for USB design is set up by the USB Implementers Forum (USB-IF). The current version (3.0) is backward compatible with older versions like 2.0, 1.1, 1.0, and 0.9.

1.5.2 Storage Devices

A storage device can record and/or store information (data). Recording is performed using any form of energy, for example, electromagnetic energy. A storage device can hold and/or process information. A device that can only hold information is referred to as a recording medium. Devices that process information (also known as data storage equipment) may access both a separate portable (removable) recording medium or a permanent component to store and retrieve information.

Electric power is required to place data in electronic data storage, which can be used both for storage and retrieval of data. This data can be stored in both analog and digital form. Most electronic data storage media are considered as permanent or nonvolatile storage, and so the data remains stored even after power is switched off. In contrast, electronically stored information is considered volatile memory.

The two main technologies available for storage are magnetic storage and optical storage. Storage devices will be discussed at length in Chapter 9. Storage in clouds, which entails digital data storage in logical pools whose physical environment is owned and managed by hosting companies, is also in vogue.

1.5.3 Input and Output Devices

An input device is a hardware mechanism that sends information from the outside world to the computer, whereas an output device is hardware used to communicate the result of data processing carried out either by the CPU or the user.

Input devices can be classified based on the modality of the input (e.g., audio, visual, and so on,) whether discrete or continuous, and the number of degrees of freedom accessible by the device. Examples include keyboards, pointing devices (e.g., mouse, joystick, touchscreen, and so on,) wired gloves, scanners, and microphones for audio. Output devices for audio are amplifiers and speakers. Other output devices include monitors, videodisc players, projectors, and printers.

Printers commonly used are inkjet printers and laser printers. *Inkjet printers* propel droplets of ink onto paper to create digital images. Inkjet printers are made from three types of technologies: (1) continuous, (2) thermal, and (3) piezoelectric. In *laser printers*, the images are produced by direct scanning of the laser beam across the printer's photoreceptor. A raster line or scan line is a horizontal strip of dots across the page. The image is produced by a raster image processor, which produces a raster image known as a bitmap that is sent to an output device for printing.

1.5.4 Communication Devices

Multimedia applications require collaboration between designers, writers, artists, musicians, and so on, in addition to clients. This is where communication devices come into play. Examples include modems, ISDNs, and cable modems.

Several communication devices are available for video interfacing, as described below.

1.5.4.1 HDMI and DVI

Present-day video interfaces to televisions and computers use high-definition multimedia interface (HDMI), digital visual interface (DVI), or DisplayPort [18]. VGA was used earlier, but it is an analog signal and so it has been replaced by HDMI, DVI, or DisplayPort connections, which are all digital connections. The similarities between HDMI and DVI include pixel resolution potentials of 1920 × 1080/60 and same transition minimized differential signaling (TMDS) standards. Conversion between HDMI and DVI can be performed using an adaptor cable. When a monitor is being used, HDMI is the input.

The advantages of HDMI include ease of use. It also cheap. HDMI is also the first choice for plugging a computer into TV. However, TVs have HDMI 1.4 connections that max out at 3820 × 2160 pixel resolution at 30 frames per second (fps). For a 4K monitor, this version is limited to 30 fps. However, 60 fps is possible for HDMI 2.0. The most recent version of HDMI (2.1) can support 8K60 and 4K120, and this version claims to reach transmission speeds of up to 10K with very high fps.

HDMI connectors use 19 pins and come in three sizes: Type A is the standard HDMI, type B is the mini HDMI, and type C is the micro HDMI.

For very high resolutions and frame rates, alternate options like DVI and DisplayPort should be explored. DisplayPort is a computer connection format capable of 3840 × 2160 pixel resolution at 60 fps for version 1.2 and multistream transport feature. DisplayPort is not recommended for connecting a computer to a monitor. It carries audio signals, and prices are the same as HDMI. Display Port has 20 pins and comes in two sizes: DisplayPort and mini DisplayPort. The most recent version is 1.4. DisplayPort is suitable for gaming applications.

Video signal over DVI is the same as that for HDMI. The maximum resolution potential for single-link hardware is the same, that is, 1920 × 1200, but dual-link can perform better. It does not carry audio and thus is not suitable for TV, but it can be used for computers without speakers.

Finally, the older interface VGA (also known as PC-RGB or D-sub15) is an analog signal that has high resolution and frame rates. However, pixel-perfect images are not likely with present-day monitors, so VGA is the last-resort cable. DVI 1.4 is the recent version.

HDMI is most suitable for consumer electronics and the first choice for TVs. It can also be used for computers. DVI can be used for computers when audio is not a consideration. DisplayPort is used for gaming purposes.

1.5.5 Multimedia Workstation

A multimedia workstation is a computer with special capabilities for handling multimedia objects like audio, video, image, and graphics. The typical components of a multimedia workstation are:

- Standard processors for processing of discrete media information like:
- Main memory and secondary storage with corresponding autonomous controllers.
- Universal processor(s) for processing of data in real time (signal processors).
- Special-purpose processors designed for graphics, audio, and video media, which contain, for example, a microcode decompression method for DVI processors.
- Graphics and video adapters, which are built-in motherboards for recent versions.
- Communications adapters, for example, the asynchronous transfer mode host interface.
- Further special-purpose adapters.

1.5.6 Operating Systems for Multimedia Workstations

With the improvement of Windows operating systems, multimedia objects can be handled equally well on Macintosh and Window platforms.

1.5.7 Sound and Graphics Cards

A **sound card** (also known as an **audio card**) is an internal computer expansion card that facilitates the input and output of audio signals to and from the computer under the control of computer programs. A **video card, graphics card**, or graphics **adapter** is an *expansion card* that generates output images to a display.

Sound cards, video cards, and graphics cards are generally not used in today's computers, however. The CPUs today use core i3, i5, or i7 in lieu of the older Pentium CPUs and so we discuss these CPUs briefly.

Intel computer processors

Earlier Celeron and Pentium processors were used as CPUs in computers. They are differentiated by clock speeds, with Pentium being faster. Both processors do not have turbo boost, hyperthreading, and 3 MB cache, and they are paired with basic Intel HD510 integrated GPU. When cost is the prime consideration in selecting a computer, Celeron or Pentium (or even AMD) is the choice.

More recent CPUs are core i3, core i5, and core i7 [19]. Core i3 has a dual core with hyperthreading, so two logical processors can be attached to the OS for the physical core. This (i3 core) model has a 3–4 MB cache and Intel HD530 GPU.

Core i5 has a quadcore CPU without hyperthreading. It also has a hyperthreading feature to run at higher clock speeds. It has a 6 MB cache and Intel HD530 GPU. Core i5 is good for video editing, Photoshop and games.

Core i7 has hyperthreading, higher clock speeds and 8 MB cache.

Review

At the end of this chapter you will have learned about the following topics:

- What multimedia is and how it differs from mass media. The evolution of multimedia to digital media and the salient features of new media.
- Different categories of multimedia. Mobile technology, namely, mobile phones and smartphones as sources of multimedia platforms.
- The evolution of Web to Web 2.0 technology, which is a transition from passive use to interactive use. Web 2.0 technology includes interesting features like blogging; podcasting; and use of social media like Facebook, Twitter, and LinkedIn.
- The applications of multimedia in business and work as well as education and entertainment. Some of these applications are useful in e-commerce and other uses in education, entertainment, and communication. New services like Hulu, Netflix, and so on have revolutionized entertainment concepts. Present-day TV systems and their advantages as multimedia devices are mentioned. Telephone communications and text messaging in mobile phones are also part of the multimedia revolution.
- The building blocks of multimedia, which include static media like text and images, and streaming media like audio and video.

The different components of a multimedia system and their details: connecting devices, storage devices, input/output devices, and communications devices. Modern-day devices like HDMI, DVI, DisplayPort, and Cloud storage facilities.

What a multimedia workstation is.

Basic idea of CPUs used in today's multimedia computer systems.

Review Questions

1. What is multimedia? How is it different from mass media? What do you understand by the term *digital media*? What are the salient features of new media?
2. How can a conventional PC be enhanced to a multimedia platform?
3. Describe some of the uses of multimedia in (a) business and work and in (b) education and entertainment.
4. What are the different categories of multimedia?
5. Describe the following devices used in multimedia systems: (a) connecting devices, (b) storage devices, (c) input/output devices, (d) communications devices.
6. Describe the components of a multimedia workstation.
7. What is HDMI, DVI and DisplayPort? Describe their uses.
8. What are the building blocks of multimedia?
9. What is Web 2.0 technology/?
10. What do you understand by the term *social media*?

Multiple-Choice Questions

1. In preparing a multimedia presentation using visual modes, which of the following are involved?
   - (a) Speech, music, sound effects
   - (b) Speech, text, video
   - (c) Images graphics, animation, video, text
   - (d) Speech, text, audio
   - (e) None of the above

2. Uses of multimedia include:
   (a) Entertainment
   (b) E-commerce
   (c) Presentation of information using different multimedia elements like images, graphics, audio, video, and text
   (d) Storage and transformation of information
   (e) All of the above
3. A multimedia media system consists of
   (a) Communication devices
   (b) Storage devices
   (c) Input/output devices
   (d) All the above
   (e) None of the above
4. An input device can be classified according to
   (a) Modality of input
   (b) Whether discrete or continuous
   (c) Number of degrees of freedom accessible by the device
   (d) None of the above
   (e) All of the above
5. Output devices are based on
   (a) Magnetic technologies
   (b) Optical technologies
   (c) Semiconductor technologies
   (d) a and b
   (e) a, b, and c
6. Which of the following is not a connecting device?
   (a) IDE
   (b) SCSI
   (c) MCI
   (d) JPG
   (e) USB
7. An inkjet printer uses which of the following technologies?
   (a) Continuous inkjet
   (b) Thermal inkjet
   (c) Piezoelectric inkjet

   (d) All of the above
   (e) None of the above
8. A sound card does not have which of the following components?
   (a) ADC converter
   (b) DAC converter
   (c) CODEC converter
   (d) Input/output device for microphones and speakers
   (e) GPU
9. Which of the following operating systems can be used for multimedia?
   (a) Macintosh
   (b) Windows
   (c) Both (a) and (b)
   (d) Neither (a) nor (b)
10. VOD is used for
   (a) Storage
   (b) Transmission
   (c) Display
   (d) a and b
   (e) a, b, and c

References

1. Ralf Steinmetz, Klara Nahrstedt, *Multimedia: Computing, Communications and Applications*, Upper Saddle River, NJ: Pearson Education, 1995.
2. Ze-Nian Li and Mark S. Drew, *Fundamentals of Multimedia*, Upper Saddle River, NJ: Pearson Education, 2004.
3. NCSA, Multimedia in today's world, http://archive.ncsa.illinois.edu/Cyberia/DVE/FusionDVE/html/multimedia__page_1.html.
4. Mrinal K. Mandal, *Multimedia Signals and Systems*, Boston, MA: Kluwer Academic Publishers now part of Springer Science + Business Media, 2003.
5. Prabhat K. Andleigh and Kiran Thakrar, *Multimedia Systems Design*, Upper Saddle River, NJ: Pearson Education, India, 1996.
6. Fred Halsall, *Multimedia Communications: Applications, Networks, Protocols and Standards*, Upper Saddle River, NJ: Pearson Education, India, 2001.
7. Kay Vaughan, *Multimedia: Making It work McGraw Hill Asia*, New York: McGraw-Hill Education, 2004.

8. Lev Manovich, Lev, New media from borges to HTML., *The New Media Reader.* (Ed.), *Noah Wardrip-Fruin & Nick Montfort.* Cambridge, MA: MIT Press, 2003.
9. Geoffrey Morrison, LED LCD vs. plasma vs. LCD, 2013, https (accessed June 2018).
10. Geoffrey Morrison, 8K TV: What you need to know, 2018, https://www.cnet.com/news/8k-tv-what-you-need-to-know/ (accessed September 2018).
11. Joshua Stern, Introduction to Web 2.0 Technologies, 2002, http://www.ictliteracy.info/rf.pdf/Web2.0_Introduction.pdf (accessed June 2018).
12. Australian Communications Consumer Action Network (ACCAN), tip sheet on 'introduction to social media', https://accan.org.au/files/Tip%20Sheets/Introduction%20to%20Social%20Media.doc (accessed June 2018).
13. Carlos Alberto Scolari, Juan Miguel Aguado, Claudio Feihoo, Mobile media: Towards a definition and taxonomy of contents and applications, *i-JIM*, 6 no. 2 29–38, 2012.
14. Cydney Grannan, *What's the Difference Between Emoji and Emoticons*? https://www.britannica.com/story/whats-the-difference-between-emoji-and-emoticons (accessed September 2018).
15. Timothy Hykes: https://www.pinterest.com/timhykes/2d-motion-graphics-tutorials/ (accessed September 2018).
16. Janssen, Cory. "What is a universal serial bus (USB)?". *Techopedia.* Archived from the original on 3 January 2014. Retrieved February 12, 2014.
17. Jan Axelson, *USB Complete: The Developer's Guide, Fifth Edition*, Madison, WI: Lakeview Research LLC, 2015, 1–7.
18. Geoffrey Morrison, HDMI vs. DisplayPort vs. DVI vs. VGA: Which connection to choose? https://www.cnet.com/news/hdmi-vs-displayport-vs-dvi-vs-vga-which-connection-to-choose/ (accessed June 2018).
19. Andrew Cunningham, Intel launches three Core M CPUs, promises more Broadwell "early 2015", Ars Technica, January 2015 (accessed October 2018).

2

Text in Multimedia

2.1 Introduction

Text is the basic form of written communication. It includes characters like letters; numbers; punctuation marks; and special symbols like *, &, ^, %, and so on. These characters are combined into words, sentences, and paragraphs to convey basic multimedia information [1–5]. Texts in the form of words, sentences, and paragraphs are used to convey thoughts, ideas, and facts in our everyday life [3].

Multimedia products depend on text for many things:

- Text is the easiest form of communication; thus, it provides a means to explain the functioning of different applications.
- Navigation through the application is facilitated using text.
- Text provides the information regarding the application.

The building blocks of text are elements like *letters, numbers* and *special characters* into, words, sentences, paragraphs, articles/chapters and even books [3,4]. These elements are [1,5]:

- Alphabet characters: A–Z
- Numbers: 0–9
- Special characters: **punctuation** [. , ; '…] and **signs** and **symbols** [* & ^ % $ £ ! /\ ~ # @ …] are called **character sets.**
- **Icons** or **drawing symbols, mathematical symbols, Greek letters,** and so on

Text can be classified as *linear* when the navigation proceeds in a sequential manner and *nonlinear* when navigation with the help of links to a desired item [2].

In digital form, an image of a text character is called a glyph.

2.2 Typefaces and Fonts

2.2.1 Typefaces

The graphic representations of letters, numbers, and special character, usually vary by type sizes and styles. These representations are referred to as typefaces [1,2,5].

The size of typefaces is measured in **points.** One point is 1/72″, or 0.0138″. It is the measuring distance from the top of capital letters like A or P to the bottom of the descenders in letters like y, p, and q.

A few effects used in typefaces that are useful for bringing readers' attention to content are listed below:

- Case: UPPER CASE and lower case;
- **Bold**, *Italic*, Underline;
- ^{superscript} or $_{\text{subscript}}$; e.g. $^{n}C_{r}$
- Emboss e.g. Emboss or shadow e.g. **Shadows;**
- Color
- Strikethrough ~~inch~~;

A font [1,2,5] is a collection of characters of single size and style belonging to a typeface family.

Although the words *typeface* and *font* are often used interchangeably, *font* can be thought of as a piece of instruction/software that tells the printer/computer what the printed character should look like. There are two classes of fonts: **serif** and **sans serif**.

Serif fonts use ornate additions like tips or flags at the ends of a letter strokes, but sans serif fonts don't have these features. Serif fonts are usually used for documents or screens that have large quantities of text because the serif helps guide the reader's eye along the text. For computer displays, sans serif fonts are considered better because of the sharper contrast. Examples of serif and sans serif fonts are shown in Figures 2.1 and 2.2.

abcdefghijklmnopqrstuvwkyz	Latin Modern Sans
abcdefghijklmnopqrstuvwkyz	Liberation Sans
abcdefghijklmnopqrstuvwkyz	Arimo
abcdefghijklmnopqrstuvwkyz	FreeSans
abcdefghijklmnopqrstuvwkyz	Nimbus Sans L
abcdefghijklmnopqrstuvwkyz	Tex Gyre Heros
abcdefghijklmnopqrstuvwkyz	Droid Sans
abcdefghijklmnopqrstuvwkyz	Roboto
abcdefghijklmnopqrstuvwkyz	Noto
abcdefghijklmnopqrstuvwkyz	Bitstream Vera Sans
abcdefghijklmnopqrstuvwkyz	DejaVu Sans

FIGURE 2.1
Examples of sans serif fonts. (By Zazpot-own work, CC.BY-SA 3.0, https://commons.wikimedia.org/windex.php?curid=60466980.)

Hello World

FIGURE 2.2
An example of a serif (Brixton-tc) font prepared using software. (From https://fontmeme.com/ffonts/brixton-tc-font/tom@tomchalky.com.)

The example in Figure 2.3 shows text in a serif font to illustrate some characteristics of text. The different features are explained below:

- The **ascender** is an upstroke on a character.
- The **descender** is a downstroke below the baseline of a character.
- **Leading** is defined as the spacing above and below a line of text, or line spacing.
- **Tracking** is defined as the spacing between characters.
- **Kerning** is defined as the deletion of space between pairs of characters, usually creating an overlap for an improvement in appearance.

Leading, tracking, and kerning examples are shown in Figures 2.4 and 2.5. The figure on the left of Figure 2.4 shows two unkerned letters A and v with tight tracking. The figure on the right shows the same letters, but they are now kerned with loose tracking.

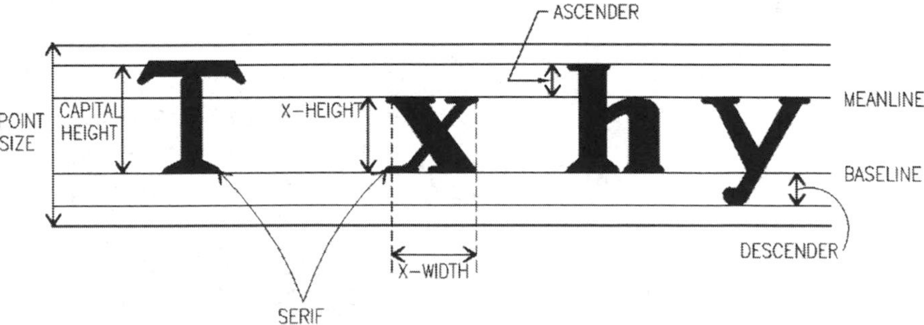

FIGURE 2.3
Example of serif text with different features labeled.

FIGURE 2.4
Examples of tracking and kerning.

FIGURE 2.5
Example of leading.

2.3 Storage of Fonts

Fonts can either be stored as **bitmapped** or **vector** graphics, as shown in Figure 2.6. Bitmap fonts depend to the size and the pixel numbers, so file size increases as more samples are added. Vector fonts, on the other hand, can draw any size by scaling the vector drawing primitives mathematically. In the figure, the file size is much smaller than bitmaps. **TrueType** and **PostScript** are vector font formats.

Distortion of characters at the edges (often referred to as jagged edges) is called aliasing. This can occur on all pixels representing characters or images. *Anti-aliasing* is the technique of making edges smooth. This has the effect of enhancing the readability and aesthetics of the text. Examples of jagged text and anti-aliased text are shown in Figure 2.7.

FIGURE 2.6
Example of bitmap and vector font. (From www.kisspng.com/png-bitmap-canopy-vector-5156946.)

FIGURE 2.7
Jagged text and anti-aliased text.

2.4 Aspects of Text Design: Ways to Represent Text

Text in multimedia should be designed to represent text in a visually appealing manner. In addition, design considerations include the providing of controls, support of keyboard interaction, and offering choice to the user [1,2,5].

The common data encoding schemes for text representing text are:

- **Plain text**, or American Standard Code for Information Interchange (ASCII) text, is text in an electronic format that can be read and interpreted by humans.
- **Rich text** embeds special control characters into the plain text to provide additional features.
- **Hypertext** is an improvement over rich text that allows the reader to jump to different sections within the document or even jump to a new document.

2.4.1 Plain Text

This is plain text. It is readable by humans. Such text contains numbers (01234) and punctuation and characters (. , # @ * &) since it uses the ASCII character set.

2.4.2 Rich Text

This is <bold>rich text</bold>.
<center>...</center>. In addition to being readable by humans, it contains additional tags that control the presentation of the text.

2.4.3 Hypertext

This is <a href= "http://www.w3c.org/">hypertext</a>. It uses the rich text format shown above but adds the ability to hyperlink to other documents and incorporate images using, for instance, <img src= "logo.gif">.

The following are considerations and guidelines to consider when working with text:

- Be concise.
- Use the appropriate typefaces and fonts.
- Make it readable.
- Consider type styles and colors.
- Use restraint and be consistent.

In addition, design considerations include the providing of controls, support of keyboard interaction, and offering choice to the user.

Figure 2.7 shows an example each of a vector font which has been anti-aliased, and a bitmapped font with jagged edges.

2.5 Effective Use of Text

Some examples of the effective use of text follow:

- Communicating data in business, such as customer names and addresses, pricing information of products.
- Explaining concepts and ideas in different fields, for example, a company mission statement or a comparison of medical procedures.
- Clarifying other media using labels on buttons, icons, and screens, and captions and callouts for graphics.
- Developing web pages, computer-based training, video, and presentations.
- Explaining the rules, chat, character descriptions, dialogue, and instructions in gaming. Education games also benefit from text

representation for content, directions, feedback, and information. Multimedia kiosks display descriptions, directions, and information using text.

- Watermarking for copyright protection, safety, and so on.

2.6 The Advantages and Disadvantages of Text

2.6.1 Advantages

- Text is relatively inexpensive to produce compared to other forms of multimedia and was the original media for computers and mobile phones.
- It can present abstract ideas effectively because words can be used generously to convey meanings at length.
- Text can be used in conjunction with other media for greater clarification.
- It provides greater confidentiality than other media because encryption and decryption is easier.
- It can be easily changed, modified, or updated.

2.6.2 Disadvantages

- Text does not have as much audiovisual impact and is thus less memorable than other visual media.
- It requires more attention because it less memorable than other media.
- It is cumbersome.

2.7 Codes and Character Sets

Multimedia information is stored and processed within a computer. For text, this is a string of characters entered in a keyboard. Each character is represented by a unique combination of a fixed number of bits known as a codeword [4]. Complete text consists of a string of codewords. Different codewords exist for different languages. There are also different character sets, for example, ASCII, mosaic.

The ASCII character set has the following features:

- Each character is represented by a unique 7-bit codeword; 7 bits means 128 (27) alternate characters and codewords used to identify each character. Hence, M (uppercase) is obtained by combining corresponding column (bits 7-5) and row (bits 4-1) bits together. Bit 7: MSB and hence the codeword for the uppercase M is 1001101.
- In addition to normal alphabetic, numeric, and punctuation characters, collectively referred to as printable characters, the total ASCII character set includes control characters, which are described in Table 2.1. Some are listed below:
  - Format control characters: backspace (BS), linefeed (LF), carriage return (CR), space (SP), delete (DEL), escape (ESC), form feed (FF)
  - Information separators: file separator (FS), record separator (RS)
  - Transmission control characters: start of heading (SOH), start of text (STX), end of text (ETX), acknowledge (ACK), negative acknowledge (NAK), synchronous idle (SYN), and data link escape (DLE)

TABLE 2.1

ASCII Character Chart Taken from an Earlier than 1972 Printer Manual (Wikipedia)

USASCII code chart

b_7 b_6 b_5 →					0 0 0	0 0 1	0 1 0	0 1 1	1 0 0	1 0 1	1 1 0	1 1 1
b_4	b_3	b_2	b_1	Row ↓ / Column →	0	1	2	3	4	5	6	7
0	0	0	0	0	NUL	DLE	SP	0	@	P	\	p
0	0	0	1	1	SOH	DC1	!	1	A	Q	a	q
0	0	1	0	2	STX	DC2	"	2	B	R	b	r
0	0	1	1	3	ETX	DC3	#	3	C	S	c	s
0	1	0	0	4	EOT	DC4	$	4	D	T	d	t
0	1	0	1	5	ENQ	NAK	%	5	E	U	e	u
0	1	1	0	6	ACK	SYN	&	6	F	V	f	v
0	1	1	1	7	BEL	ETB	'	7	G	W	g	w
1	0	0	0	8	BS	CAN	(	8	H	X	h	x
1	0	0	1	9	HT	EM	)	9	I	Y	i	y
1	0	1	0	10	LF	SUB	*	:	J	Z	j	z
1	0	1	1	11	VT	ESC	+	;	K	[	k	{
1	1	0	0	12	FF	FS	,	<	L	\	l	|
1	1	0	1	13	CR	GS	–	=	M	]	m	}
1	1	1	0	14	SO	RS	.	>	N	^	n	~
1	1	1	1	15	SI	US	/	?	O	—	o	DEL

2.8 Unicode

A universal character set that defines all characters needed for writing most living languages in use on computers is referred to as UNICODE. Unicode uses a 16-bit architecture for multilingual text and character encoding. The Unicode consortium is a nonprofit organization that develops and maintains the Unicode standard worldwide.

Unicode provides a unique number for every character regardless of platform, program, or language. Significant cost savings over the use of a legacy character set can be achieved by incorporating Unicode into client-server or multi-tier platforms. Thus, a single software product can be targeted across multiple platforms, languages, and countries without re-engineering or corruption.

2.9 Encryption and Decryption

Encryption is the process of encoding text (called plain text) into a form that is not understood by unauthorized people so that the sender can transmit the data (e.g., text) over the network. Decryption is the reverse process of retrieving the plain text from the encrypted text on the receiver's end.

2.10 Emoticons and Emojis

The Internet has introduced new features in text messages to convey nuanced meaning because body language or verbal tones cannot be incorporated into standard text messages. These new features include the addition of two new-age hieroglyphic languages: emoticons and the more recent emoji [6].

Emoticons, or "emotional icons," are punctuation marks, letters, and numbers used to create pictorial icons that generally display an emotion or sentiment. Their general use started in 1982. The components of an emoticon are usually generated from a keyboard. Typical emoticons are smiley faces and frowning faces.

Emojis are a slightly more recent invention. The word *emoji* originates from the Japanese word from the Japanese *e* ("picture") and *moji* ("character") and was invented by Shigetaka Kurita in 1999. Emojis are pictographs of faces, objects, and symbols. The typical Apple emoji is the yellow cartoon face with various expressions.

2.11 Text in Mobile Devices

Mobile devices have small screen sizes, typically around several inches, so the viewing of text and interacting with textual content is difficult. Text must thus be allowed to reflow so that the reader scrolls down, not sideways. Reflow of text allows change of font size, thus making reading easier for users to suit their eyesight.

All ebook readers like the Amazon-based Kindle reader and Internet-enabled mobile phones and tablets support plain text and HTML. These formats reflow without any special treatment. However, formats like PDF do not allow reflow and thus prevent the copying of text. These formats allow reflow only if they've been set up to allow it. Basic Internet phones do not support PDF or e-publication (ePub). All smartphones and some feature phones might or might not support PDF and ePub. The reflow feature for PDF files can be incorporated if tagged documents are used in conjunction with instruction sets provided for use by software manufactured for this purpose. The reflow feature can improve accessibility of text from ePub and PDF documents for screen readers as well as mobile devices.

ePub is a widely adopted, open source standard for electronic books (ebooks). Distribution and interchange format standards for digital publications and documents are based on Web standards, providing a means of representing, packaging, and encoding structured and semantically enhanced Web content, including XHTML, CSS, SVG, images, and other resources for distribution in a single-file format.

Review

At the end of this chapter you will have learned about the following topics:

- What text is and the different types and characteristics of text
- Typefaces and fonts
- Storage of text as bitmap and vector fonts
- Aspects of text design
- Uses of text
- Advantages and disadvantages of text as a multimedia object
- Codes and character sets
- Unicode
- Encryption and decryption

Review Questions

1. What do you understand by the term *text*?
2. What is a typeface? What are the two main types of fonts? Give examples.
3. Describe the difference between bitmap and vector font. What is anti-aliasing?
4. Describe three ways to represent text.
5. What are the uses of text?
6. List the advantages and disadvantages of using text in multimedia.
7. Briefly describe the ASCII character set.
8. What is Unicode?
9. What do you understand by the terms *encryption* and *decryption*?

Multiple Choice Questions

1. Which of the following is *not* an alphanumeric character?
   (a) B
   (b) 3
   (c) x
   (d) %
   (e) 777
2. Which of the following is *not* a typeface effect?
   (a) Emboss
   (b) Color
   (c) Bold
   (d) Subscript
   (e) None of the above
3. Tracking is
   (a) An upstroke on a character
   (b) A downstroke below the baseline of a character
   (c) Space between characters
   (d) Space above and/or below characters
   (e) Spacing between pairs of characters

4. Bitmaps
   (a) Depend on size
   (b) Depend on pixel numbers
   (c) Require larger storage than vector fonts
   (d) All of the above
   (e) None of the above
5. Hypertext
   (a) Allows readers to jump to different portions of the document
   (b) Allows readers to jump to different documents
   (c) Has all the features of rich text
   (d) All of the above
   (e) None of the above
6. Which of the following is true of text?
   (a) It allows the communication of ideas
   (b) It explains concepts and ideas
   (c) It clarifies other media
   (d) a and b
   (e) a, b, and c
7. Text
   (a) Is inexpensive
   (b) Clarifies ideas
   (c) Is less attractive than other forms of multimedia
   (d) Is cumbersome
   (e) All of the above
8. The ASCII character set combines
   (a) Column (bits 7-5) and row (bits 4-1)
   (b) Column (bits 5-7) and row (bits 1-4)
   (c) Column (bits 4-1) and row (bits 7-5)
   (d) Column (bits 1-4) and row (bits 5-7)
   (e) None of the above
9. Unicode provides a unique number for every character for
   (a) Platform
   (b) Program
   (c) Language
   (d) All of the above
   (e) None of the above

References

1. Kay Vaughan, *Multimedia: Making It Work*, McGraw-Hill, Berkeley, CA, 2004.
2. Ralf Steinmetz and Klara Nahrstedt, *Multimedia: Computing, Communications and Applications*, Upper Saddle River, New Jersey: Pearson Education, 1995.
3. Prabhat K. Andleigh and Kiran Thakrar, *Multimedia Systems Design*, New Delhi, India: Pearson Education, 1996.
4. Fred Halsall, *Multimedia Communications: Applications, Networks, Protocols and Standards*, Pearson Education, India, 2001.
5. Text from Multimedia, https: gmm.fsksm.utm.my/.../cgi../Lecture6%20-%20 Text.ppt (accessed 2004).
6. Cydney Grannan, What's the Difference Between Emoji and Emoticons? https://www.britannica.com/story/whats-the-difference-between-emoji-and-emoticons (accessed September 2018).

3

Audio in Multimedia

3.1 Introduction

Multimedia elements like audio, video, and images try to make the virtual world of the computer more appealing to humans because they appeal to the human senses of hearing and sight [1–5]. Thus, an audiovisual representation of multimedia presentations in computers as well as mobile and smartphones would make a better impact than text, no matter how ornamental the text. Hence, audio, which is a representation of sound in the form of sound or periodic audio signals, and, of course, music enhance the multimedia experience. Multimedia should consist of at least one static element like text or image as well as a streaming or temporal element like audio. Even the impact of text can be enhanced with background music. Hence, the study of sound is essential for the understanding of audio.

Audio is a result of the propagation of longitudinal mechanical waves (which are sound waves) generated because of periodic compressions and rarefactions produced in the media of propagation (generally air). These pressure fluctuations become perceptible as audio or sound waves to humans when the frequency of these periodic disturbances is above a certain minimum value (20 cycles/sec, or 20 Hertz [Hz]). When the frequency exceeds a maximum value of 20,000 Hz, these waves are called ultrasound waves, which are beyond the range of human hearing. Humans can hear frequencies in range 20–20,000 Hz. Acoustics is the branch of physics that studies sound. The propagation of sound waves can occur only in the presence of a material medium such as air. In following sections, we will elaborate on the physical properties of audio and sound. In multimedia, audio is classified as a temporal object that includes streaming data.

3.2 Characteristics of Audio

Audio is essentially a sound wave; thus, it has normal wave properties like reflection, refraction, and diffraction. A sound wave is characterized by the following physical properties, which will be described in more detail below [1–6]:

- *Amplitude (loudness/intensity)*: Sound waves can be represented graphically in two dimensions, with time along the independent (x) axis and amplitude along the dependent (y) axis. Sound waves are periodic compressions alternated with rarefactions propagated in time. The square of the amplitude is the intensity. This gives a measure, known as bel, of the loudness of sound in an appropriate dimension.
- *Frequency (pitch)*: Frequency gives a measure of the rapidity at which the periodic variations of compression and rarefaction occur and is a measure of the pitch of the sound. A high pitch corresponds to high-frequency sound, and vice versa.
- *Envelope (waveform)*: The evolution of the sound until it dies down generates a form or envelope.

3.2.1 Audio Amplitude

The amplitude of a sound or an audio wave is a measure of the range of variation during each cycle of vibration. The maximum amplitude corresponds to the crest of the wave, representing the maximum disturbance (also known as the antinode) and the waveform goes through zero disturbance (node) to a maximum negative amplitude, referred to as trough (antinode).

Audio amplitude is often expressed in decibels (dB), which is the sound intensity, a quantity proportional to the square of the amplitude. Sound pressure levels expressed in terms of loudness or volume are measured on a logarithmic scale (dB) used to describe a ratio. Suppose we have two loudspeakers [2,3,6], the first playing a sound with power p_1 and another playing a louder version of the same sound with power p_2/p_1; everything else (how far away, frequency) is kept the same. The difference in decibels between the two is defined as 10 log10 (p_2) db. In microphones, audio is captured as analog signals, which are signals of continuous amplitude and time, that respond proportionally to the sound pressure, P. The power in a sound wave, all else equal, is the square of the pressure, expressed in dynes/cm^2. The sound pressure level difference between two sounds with p_1 and p_2 is given by 20 log(p_2/p_1) db. Some typical examples of loudness [2,3,6] are given in Table 3.1. The acoustic amplitude of sound is measured about $p_1 = p_{ref} =$ 0.0002 dynes/cm^2. The threshold of the human ear corresponds to sound pressure levels below p_{ref}, below which it is insensitive.

TABLE 3.1

Typical Sound Intensities

Intensity in Decibels	Examples
0	Threshold of hearing
10	Rustling of leaves
20–25	Typical ambient level of a recording studio or quiet room
40–45	Typical ambient level in a normal room
60–70	Conversation level
60–70	Busy street
80	Noise due to heavy road traffic
90	Train going through a station
120–130	Threshold of pain
140	Rock singer screaming into microphone
160	Damage to eardrum

3.2.2 Audio Frequency

The frequency, or number of cycles per second of sound waves, range of sounds [2–4,6] can be divided into the categories shown in the following chart:

Infra sound	0 Hz–20 Hz	This range is for no sound to sound below the audible range of humans.
Audible sound	20 Hz–20 KHz	This is the range for normal human hearing.
Ultrasound	20 KHz–1 GHz	This range is beyond the range of human hearing but audible for bats.
Hyper sound	1 GHz–10 GHz	This range corresponds to supersonic sound.

Sound waves propagate with a typical speed of around 344 m/s in humid air at room temperature (20°C) Hence, audio wavelengths typically vary from 17 m (corresponding to 20 Hz) to 1.7 cm (corresponding to 20 KHz). Sound can be divided into periodic, which includes natural phenomena like whistling wind or the singing of birds, songs, and music, and nonperiodic, which include natural phenomena like sneezing and rushing water and even speech. Natural sounds are combinations of different frequencies and wave shapes. The spectrum of a typical audio signal has one or more fundamental frequencies, their harmonics, and possibly a few cross-modulation products.

Fundamental frequency, also known as the first harmonic, is the lowest frequency produced by an instrument. Harmonics are higher multiples of the fundamental frequency, and their amplitudes determine the *tone quality* or *timbre.*

3.2.3 Audio Envelope

The duration of generated sound is finite, and its rise and fall in intensity constitutes an envelope, as depicted in Figure 3.1. A typical envelope [2,3,6] consists of four sections: attack, decay, sustain, and release; thus it is called the ADSR envelope.

Attack: Occurs when the intensity of a note increases from silence to a high level right after the generation of sound.

Decay: Occurs when the intensity decreases to a middle level.

Sustain: Is manifested when the middle level is sustained for a short period of time.

Release: Occurs when the intensity drops from the sustain level to zero after the removal of the sound source.

Different instruments have different envelope shapes, for example, the violin and cello (that is, bowed string instrument) produce notes that have slower attacks but a longer sustain period. The guitar and sitar (plucked string instruments) produce notes that have quick attacks and slower release.

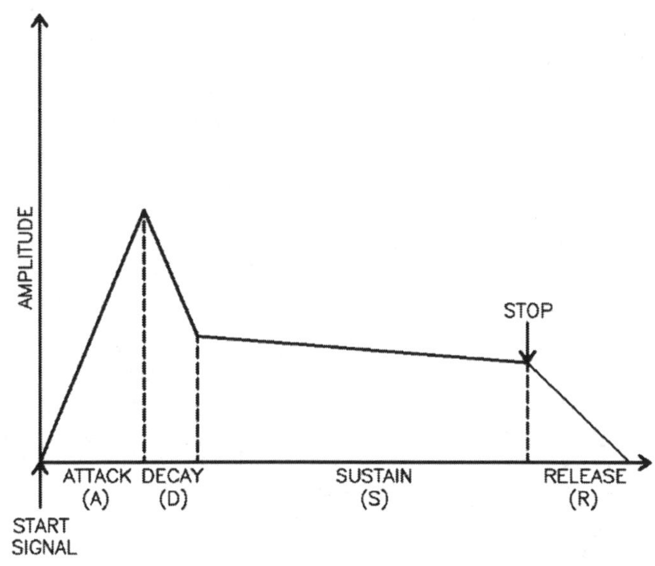

FIGURE 3.1
Audio envelope (ADSR envelope).

3.3 Digitization of Audio Samples

Sound is generated as a continuous signal, also known as the an analog signal. To generate audio data in a computer, however, this signal needs to be digitized. This process takes place in two stages: sampling and quantization [4,7].

The input streaming audio data in a computer for use as a multimedia object, the continuous audio wave (analog signal) needs to be digitized to the discrete output signal. This takes place in two stages, as described below.

3.3.1 Sampling

As input audio signals are continuous in time and amplitude, they must be digitized in both time and amplitude. This is necessary for the signal to be represented in binary form. Sampling in time involves taking amplitude values of the signal at discrete time intervals. The frequency of sampling or the number of times the sampling is carried out is determined by the Nyquist theorem. This theorem states that, for a signal that is band limited, that is, has lower and upper bounds of frequency, the sampling rate should be at least twice the bandwidth. Quantization refers to the process of taking the amplitude values of the signal at these time intervals.

- Discretized in time by sampling at the Nyquist rate, which is the sampling rate that is at least twice the highest frequency of the sample.
- Discretized in amplitude by quantization: After capturing samples have been captured at discrete time intervals, they must be discretized in amplitude.

3.3.2 Quantization

Quantization converts actual amplitude sample values, which are usually voltage measurements, into an integer approximation. This is the process of rounding off a continuous value so that it can be represented by a fixed number of binary digits. This results in error due to the trade-off between the number of bits required and the actual value.

The quantization process is described as follows. The sample value is rounded off to the closest integer (e.g., round 5.26 to 5). An audio signal with a voltage range between –10 V and +10 V is considered. The audio waveform has already been time sampled, as shown in Figure 3.2. One can represent each sample by four bits. There are an infinite number of voltages between –10 V and 10 V. A range of voltages is assigned to each

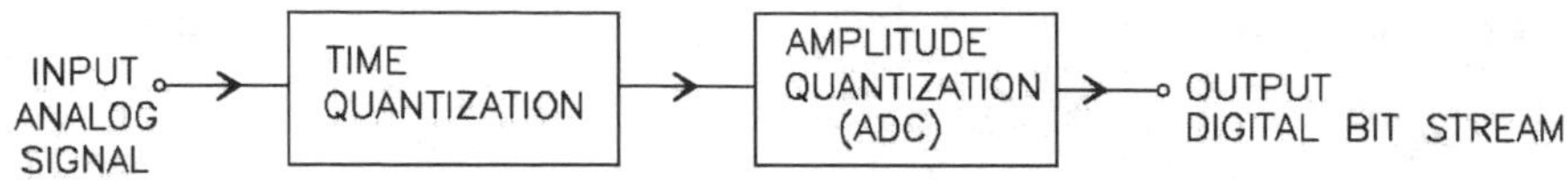

FIGURE 3.2
The two-step digitization process.

four-bit codeword. There will be 16 steps. The step size is computed as follows (see Figure 3.3):

$$\frac{10-(-10)}{16}=1.25\text{V}.$$

A table like the one in Table 3.2 is generated and shows a staircase pattern of values.

3.3.3 Example of Sampling and Quantization in Compact Discs (CDs)

3.3.3.1 Sampling

Recording studios conform to the audio industry standard for highest frequency of 20 kHz. The Nyquist sampling rate is 40 kHz. To be on the safe side, the audio industry oversamples to 44,100 cycles per second.

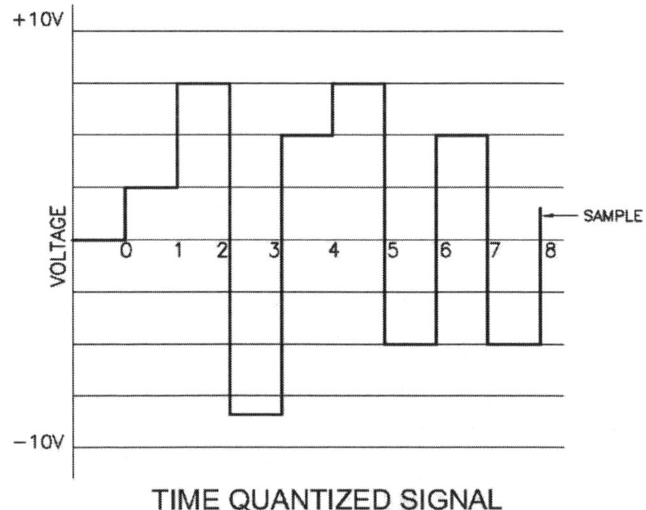

FIGURE 3.3
The quantized audio signal.

TABLE 3.2

Code Values of Voltage Bins

Range	Code	Range Center
8.75 → 10.0	1111	9.375
7.50 → 8.75	1110	8.125
6.25 → 7.50	1101	6.875
5.0 → 6.25	1100	5.625
3.75 → 5.0	1011	4.375
2.50 → 3.75	1010	3.125
1.25 → 2.50	1001	1.875
0.0 → 1.25	1000	0.625
−1.25 → 0.0	0111	−0.625
−2.5 → −1.25	0110	−1.875
−3.75 → −2.5	0101	−3.125
−5.0 → −3.75	0100	−4.375
−6.25 → −5.0	0011	−5.625
−7.5 → −6.25	0010	−6.875
−8.75 → −7.5	0001	−9.375
−10.0 → −8.75	0000	9.375

Source: USUP State faculty Lecture notes, http://faculty.uscupstate.edu/.../DigitalAudio_Chapter12.ppt.

The sampling size is the bit-depth, which is the number of bits per sample (also known as bit resolution). The sampling rate is the number of samples per second.

3.3.3.2 Quantization

CDs have 16 bits to represent each sample, thus totaling 65,536 possible samples on one CD. Each channel is converted into bits at a rate of 44,100 samples/sec * 16 bits/sample = 705,600 bits/sec. Thus, 60 minutes * 60 secs/min * 705 600 bits/sec * 2 channels (stereo) = 5 080 320 000 bits = 605.62 MB, which is about the size of a CD.

3.3.3.3 Reconstruction

An analog-to-digital converter (ADC) converts the continuous signal to the sampled and quantized binary code. A digital-to-analog converter (DAC) reverts the quantized binary code to an approximation of the analog signal (reverses the quantization process) by clocking the code to the same sample rate as the ADC conversion.

An example of both quantization and reconstruction is shown in Figure 3.4.

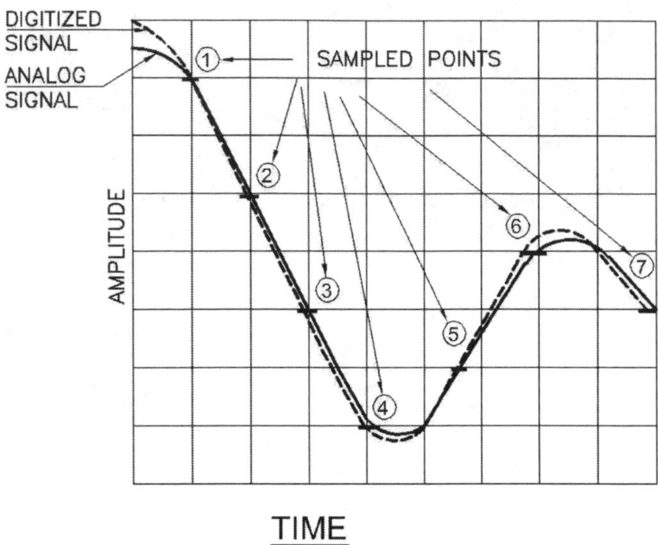

FIGURE 3.4
Quantization and reconstruction.

3.3.3.4 Quantization Error

In Figure 3.4, the sampled points and small horizontal lines indicate the points where the samples are taken and quantized to the y value of the grid. Figure 3.4 also shows the reconstructed signal (unbroken lines) using these values. The original signal is also superposed with dashed lines. It is found that quantization is only an approximation and that some information is lost, thereby introducing some error.

The difference between the original sample value and the rounded value is termed the quantization error. A signal to noise ratio (SNR) is defined as the ratio of the relative sizes of the signal values and the errors. The higher the SNR, the smaller the average error is with respect to the signal value and the better the fidelity.

3.4 Fourier Analysis

Sound waves occurring in nature are usually complex signals comprising simple waves of different frequencies [7]. For further analysis and processing, these signals need to be broken down into their constituent simple waves. The Fourier transform performs the operation of breaking down a complex signal into its constituent waves.

A mechanical wave, such as compressions and rarefactions of sound pressure, or the output sine voltage of an amplifier can be represented as a continuous function of time. A pure tone produces a sound pressure proportional to $f(t) = \sin(\omega o t)$, which corresponds to the *time domain* representation of the sound. There is an equivalent *frequency domain* representation of a pure tone.

The frequency domain representation is more for filter design and analysis, among other applications. The magnitude of this function is normally termed the frequency response. The phase is equally important and must also be specified to give a complete frequency domain representation. A Fourier transform (FT) pair is a mathematical relation converting the time (t) to frequency (ω) domain representations, and converting frequency to time for the inverse case, as shown below.

$$F(\omega) = \int_{-\infty}^{\infty} f(t)\exp(-j\omega t)dt$$

$$f(t) = \frac{1}{2\pi}\int_{-\infty}^{\infty} F(\omega)\exp(-j\omega t)d\omega$$

A natural sound signal is a combination of several simple waves, for example, sine waves. A complex waveform can be generated from a series of simple waveforms. Analysis of these waveforms can be performed using Fourier analysis. The Fourier transform helps in analyzing a signal in a domain that is different from its original domain.

3.5 Sub-band Coding

Sub-band coding (SBC) breaks up a signal into several frequency bands [7] by using a fast Fourier transform (FFT) and encodes each band independently. SBC is the first step in the compression of audio and video signals. It is used in lossy as well as lossless compression. Compression of signals entails the decrease in the size of the signals using coding techniques. When some information is eliminated permanently by the coding technique, the compression is termed lossy; an example is MP3. When the coding techniques enables the retrieval of the complete signal, the scheme is a lossless compression.

As mentioned in the previous section, filters are used for various applications in audio. A *filter* is system that isolates certain frequencies. An audio source output can be decomposed into its constituent parts using digital filters. The source is made up of constituent parts, each of which are the different bands of frequencies making up the source. SBC is a compression approach where digital filters are used to separate the source output into different bands of frequencies. Each part then can be encoded separately.

3.6 Music

One of the important applications of audio in multimedia is in the use of music [8–10]. The advent of electronic musical instruments, like the synthesizer in the 1960s, heralded music in the digital domain. Even recording and representations using audio CDs were part of this digital revolution, which also saw the entry of radio station archives stored in digital discs.

The technology that helped in the digitization of music was pulse code modulation (PCM) in telecommunication, as well as motion picture experts group (MPEG) audio in multimedia systems, whereby coding, compression, and transmission of digital sound were made possible. The introduction of musical instrument digital interface (MIDI) enabled the exchange of musical instrument data over digital links.

Music elicits emotions as well as arousal of the senses from listeners. Listening to specific types of music can result in improvement of spatial learning. Hence, music in multimedia can enhance the teaching-learning process.

In entertainment, media presentations are made using both visual and auditory media; these are known as formal features. Although visual features are essential for rendering a presentation that will capture the attention of the audience, auditory features in the form of music can arouse emotions. The auditory feature forms a synergistic compliment to visual features.

Music is one of the most important aspects for the purposes of online video marketing. Music sets the tone. If the presentation is aimed at providing detailed information on a product, say, then subtle background music can help the audience in concentrating on the material presented without much distraction. Music libraries can also help in making choices for setting the tone. Some examples of such libraries are www.bedracks.com with Sonic Search, SoundStripe.com, and premiumbeat.com. Efforts should also be made to mix the tracks. There are many free software tools for video editing that have a set of mixing tools. Ideally, the sound level of these video presentations should be below −6 db.

This section discusses some characteristics of musical sound. Musical sound is generated by musical notes, which are sound waves of fixed frequencies (fundamental notes or first harmonics) or their multiples (higher harmonics) These notes range from A to G, and their solfeges, which is singing using solfa syllables to denote the notes of the scale, for example, do, re, mi or sa, re, ga in Western and Indian (Hindusthani) music, are, respectively, do, re, mi, fa, so, la, ti and sa, re, ga, ma, pa, dha, ni. A set of eight notes (from C to the next higher multiple of C, or Do to the next Do, or Sa to the next Sa) is referred to as an *octave*.

The three characteristics of music are

- *Loudness*: Loudness is related to the intensity of the musical sound.
- *Pitch*: Pitch is related to the frequency.
- *Timbre*: Timbre is the tonal quality of the music and is characterized by a complex waveform.

In standard Western music notation [8], the *staff*, or *stave*, is a set of five horizontal lines and four spaces that each represent a different musical *pitch*—or, in the case of a percussion staff, different percussion instruments. Extra notes can be accommodated outside these five lines, by adding extra *leger lines* (also spelled *ledger*) where needed.

The absolute pitch of each line for a non-percussive stave is determined by the placement of an appropriate *clef* symbol at the appropriate vertical position on the left-hand side of the staff. The *treble clef* (Figure 3.5), also known as the G clef, is placed on the second line (counting upward), fixing that line as the pitch first G above *middle* C. The *bass clef*, sometimes called the F clef because the two dots are centered on the line for note F, is also shown in Figure 3.5. The numbering of lines and spaces start from bottom to top; the bottom line is the *first line*, while the top line is the *fifth line*. The relationship between timing counts is indicated by a *time signature* to the right of the clef. *Bar lines* are used to group notes on the staff into *measures*. A time signature, or meter signature, refers to beats per measure. A bar, or measure, is defined

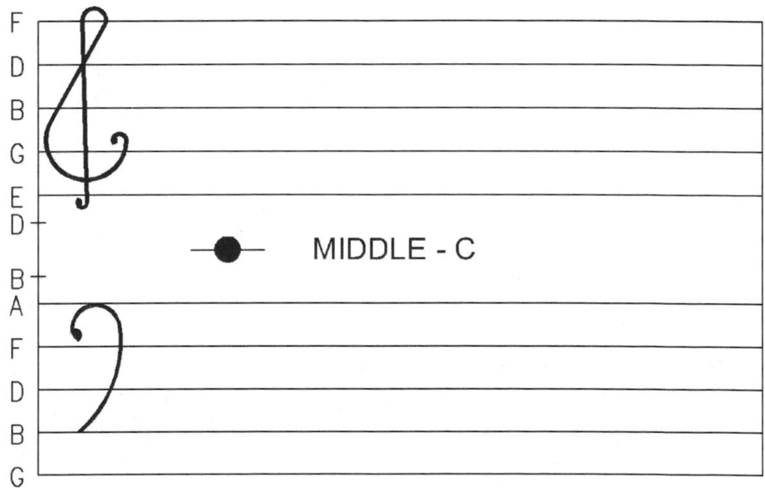

FIGURE 3.5
Staff notation and clefs.

as a segment of time defined by a given number of beats of a given duration. The treble and bass clef together comprise a pair that cover a wider range of notes that fit together conveniently with a single leger line, used for middle C, between them. This is known as a *grand stave* (Figure 3.5), and the treble and bass staves are always joined with a vertical line at the left end to show that they belong together.

Singing voices can be broadly classified into four categories based on the frequency range of the voice:

- Soprano (female voice) ranges from middle C to high A or soprano C, two octaves above middle C.
- Alto (female or male voice) ranges from G below middle C to F in second octave above middle C.
- Tenor (male voice) ranges from one octave below middle C to A above middle C.
- Bass (male voice) starts from second E below middle C to E above middle C.

The two methods for representing an audio signal are the waveform and the parametric methods. Music synthesis uses parametric method. The waveform method will be discussed in the context of MIDI. Parametric methods for music synthesis hinge on the use of the octave chart. Speech uses parametric methods.

3.6.1 Digital Sound Synthesis

Computers store digitized sound [9], but the audience hears analog sound. Hence, digitized sound or sampled audio needs to be converted to an analog signal. Two basic approaches are frequency modulation (FM) and wavetable, or wave. The resulting output is referred to as synthetic sound.

In FM, a second modulating frequency is added to the argument of the main cosine term, which corresponds to the carrier sinusoid. This results in having a term that is the cosine of the cosine. An envelope function, which is essentially a time varying amplitude, multiplies the whole signal. A second time-varying amplitude multiplies with the inner cosine term to account for the overtones. A couple of extra constants are added to produce a resulting complex signal. FM synthesis is good for producing simple music.

Another technique for digitizing is by wavetable synthesis. Digitized samples are stored sound from digital instruments. Wavetables are stored in memory and can be operated by software for combining, editing, and enhancing the sound. Some memory space-saving techniques can be used. Examples of these techniques include sample looping, pitch shifting, mathematical interpolation, and polyphonic digital filtering. Wavetable synthesis can be used to accurately real instrument sounds in musical instrument digital interface (MIDI), which is discussed in the next section.

3.7 MIDI

MIDI is a technology that allows electronic musical instruments to communicate with each other by sending and receiving performance information. By performance information, we mean pressing a key on the piano or plucking the string of a guitar. This performance information constitutes the MIDI data, which can be saved to a file or transmitted to another musical instrument for later playback.

MIDI is a scripting language and at the same time a hardware setup. As a scripting language, MIDI can code events like pitch of a single note and its duration and volume. Hence MIDI files are small. The MIDI data on a computer can be edited. Multiple MIDI devices can be interconnected to transmit and receive data. Generally, a MIDI cable is used for connecting an instrument to another instrument, and a USB cable is used for connecting instruments to a computer. MIDI data has a two advantages over audio data:

- The size of the data is much smaller than conventional audio data such as MP3, WAV, and so on.
- The data can be edited effectively and easily.

The data stream of MIDI originates from a MIDI controller such as a MIDI sequencer or keyboard. The MIDI stream is received by the MIDI sound generator or sound module. A diagram of a MIDI system is given in Figure 3.6.

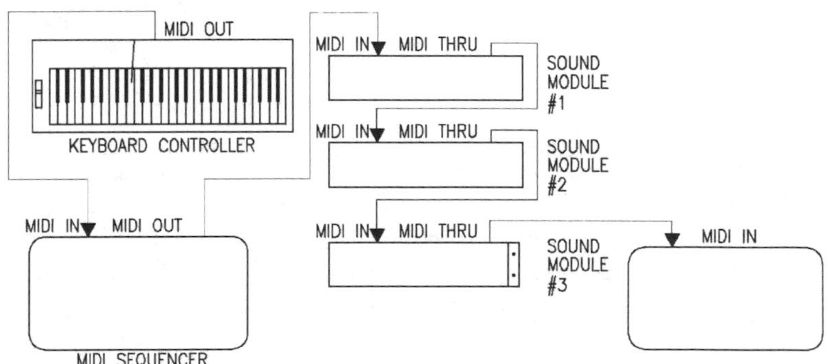

FIGURE 3.6
Diagram of a MIDI system.

3.7.1 MIDI Channels

MIDI performance data are assigned to one of 16 MIDI channels identified by including a four-bit channel number with the MIDI message. A typical MIDI message constitutes a status byte, followed by one or two bytes of data. Using these channels, 1–16, the performance data for 16 different instrument parts can be sent simultaneously over one cable. Thus, when a song is played on the keyboard, the song contains many parts—right-hand part, left-hand part, rhythm part, bass part, and so on. For the instruments supported by MIDI, different channels are assigned automatically to each instrument. Thus, for a MIDI song to be transmitted to another instrument through a MIDI cable, each part is transmitted simultaneously over separate channels. MIDI data, or messages, can be divided into two groups: channel messages and system messages.

- *Channel messages:* Channel messages are generated when an instrument is played. For example, while playing the keyboard, some messages generated include note on/off (when the keyboard was played/released), note number (which key was played), and velocity (indicating how strongly the key was played). For selecting a voice, the program change message is generated.
- *System messages:* System message consist of data that are common to the entire MIDI system. These include system exclusive messages for transferring data unique to each instrument manufacturer and real-time messages for controlling the MIDI devices. The MIDI data stream originates from a MIDI controller such as a MIDI sequencer or keyboard. The recipient of the MIDI stream is the MIDI sound generator or sound module. There are 16 logical channels that are identified by including a four-bit channel number with the MIDI.

3.7.2 MIDI Hardware

MIDI hardware consists of a sequencer, a synthesizer, and a keyboard. There is a 31.25 kbps serial connection with 10 bits, including a 0 start and stop bit. In MIDI terminology, timbre refers to the quality of sound. It is essentially the quality of the sound of the musical instrument to be emulated. Voice in MIDI is the timbre(s) and pitch(es) that the tone module can play at the same time. Polyphony refers to the number of voices that can be produced at the same time. Multi-timbral means that audio from several instruments can be produced simultaneously. Playing several notes at the same time is referred to as multi-voice.

3.7.2.1 Sequencer

A sequencer is a device to record, edit, and play back music. In a sequencer, music is organized into tracks. Each track is turned on or off on recording or playing back. A sequencer is basically a music editor. This editor can edit standard music notation as well as manipulate data. Wavetable data can also be stored in the form of WAV files, which have the advantage of being able to store the exact sound of the instrument. A sampler is used to sample the audio data before storing as wavetable files. Other specific functions include:

- Helping send MIDI messages to the MIDI synthesizer.
- Adding time-stamping to the MIDI messages.
- Volume control over time by a process known as time-varying amplitude modulation is possible.
- Time compression or expansion with no pitch change can be performed.

3.7.2.2 Synthesizer

A synthesizer is a device that electronically synthesizes sound. It can act as a stand-alone generator of sound that can vary the pitch, loudness, and tone color. Additional characteristics include the ability to change the attack and delay times. A synthesizer has a typical electronic master keyboard with a modulation wheel to add vibrato and a pitch bend wheel to alter the frequency as well as connected modules. The MIDI ports of the master keyboard consist of two five-pin connectors labeled IN and OUT and a third connector labeled THRU. Other properties include the following:

- It is polyphonic.
- It can play more than one note at a time.
- A synthesizer that can play five notes simultaneously and produce a piano sound and an acoustic bass sound at the same time is multi-timbral.

3.7.2.3 MIDI Keyboard

A MIDI keyboard produces no sound. It generates messages that consist of a few bytes. MIDI messages are described in the next section.

3.7.3 Standard MIDI Messages and Files

One instrument is associated with a MIDI channel. MIDI channels are used to separate MIDI messages. There are 16 channels numbered 0–15.

The channel forms the last four bits (least significant bits). Each channel is associated with an instrument: 1 is for piano, 10 is for percussion instrument, and so on. Even foreign instruments like the Indian sitar and shehnai (channel 104 and 111, respectively) and Japanese koto (channel 107) are included. There are two types of messages: channel messages and system messages.

A MIDI file is the major source of music in computer games and CD entertainment titles. The file format is standard MIDI format (SMF), which stores standard MIDI messages along with the appropriate timing information. SMF files organize data in chunks, preceded by an ID. A chunk is defined as a group of related data items. Each chunk begins with a four-character ID and includes information such as the type of chunk. The Tonext four bytes form the size of the chunk. ID and size form the chunk header. MIDI chunks are of two types: (1) Mthd and (2) Mtrk. The first is a header chunk; the second is a track chunk. Interested readers can consult Tutorial on MIDI and Music Synthesis by MIDI Manufacturers Association.

3.7.4 Wavetable Synthesis

Wavetable synthesis [11] is a technique for storing high-quality sound samples digitally and playing them on demand. A table of sound wave forms is prepared and stored. These may be looked up and utilized when needed, hence the name wavetable. To reduce the amount of memory required to store these samples, techniques collectively called wavetable synthesis techniques are employed. Two such techniques are outlined below.

3.7.4.1 Example of Looping and Envelope Generation (Technique I: Figures 3.7 and 3.8)

The sustain section is represented by looping the wave samples, multiplied by the gain factor, which is governed by the ADSR envelope [11]. To store a waveform, two things are required [11]:

- A sample of the attack section of the input signal
- A sample for the loop in the sustain section of the input signal

The number of samples gives a measure of the loop length. Note that a sample whose sound cannot be adequately modeled as ADSR, such as short sounds or sounds of dynamic behavior, cannot be looped. These sounds are termed *one-shot sounds.*

3.7.4.2 Pitch Shifting (Technique 2)

To generate a number of different notes from a single sound sample of a given instrument, pitch shifting [11] can be used. Pitch shifting involves

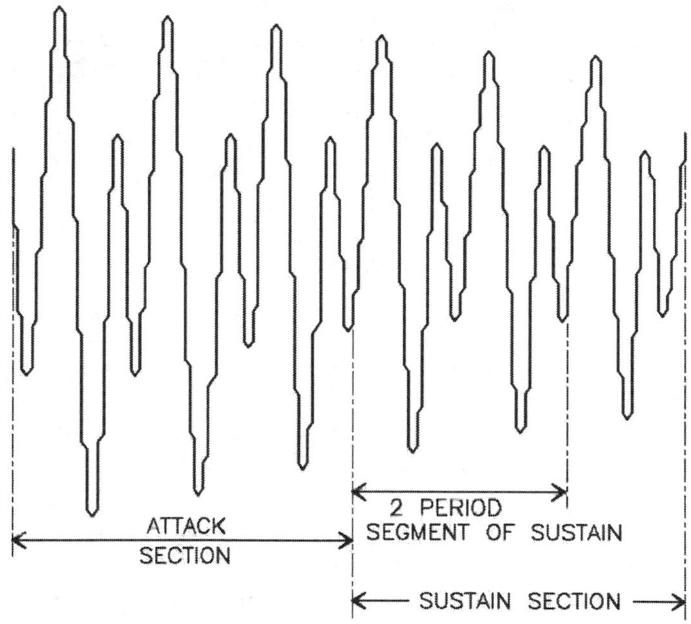

FIGURE 3.7
Attack and sustain portions of a waveform and looping of a sample segment. (From the MIDI Manufacturers Association, Tutorial: MIDI and Music Synthesis, https://www.midi.org/articles-old/tutorial-midi-and-music-synthesis-1, 1995.)

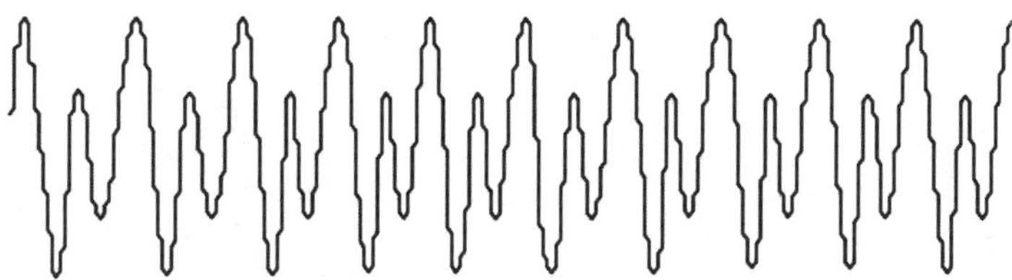

FIGURE 3.8
Waveform from looping segment. (From the MIDI Manufacturers Association, Tutorial: MIDI and Music Synthesis, https://www.midi.org/articles-old/tutorial-midi-and-music-synthesis-1, 1995.)

reading the stored sample at different rates. By allowing the sample pointer to have only integer increments, the pitch shifts are restricted to a limited set. Generally, a sample pointer consists of an integer as well as fractional pointers.

3.8 Speech Recognition and Synthesis

The ability of a machine or program to identify words and phrases in spoken language and convert them to a machine-readable format is called the speech recognition process. It is a pipeline for converting PCM [2–4] digital audio from a sound card into recognized speech.

Apply « grammar » so the speech recognizer knows what phonemes to expect. Phonemes are a finite set of abstract symbols used to annotate real sounds, referred to as phones. Grammar can be anything from context-free grammar to full-blown text. Examples of speech recognition software include ISIP Speech Recognition toolkit, Praat, and so on.

For the generation of speech to text, parameters are obtained through completely automated training on a few hours of speech data acquired by recording a prepared script. Synthesis is accomplished by concatenating very small segments of recorded human speech to produce synthesized speech. This is done using IBM/Watson Text To Speech (TTS) software (IBM's TTS s/w). Other examples of speech synthesis software are Festival and Emu.

3.9 Multi Channel and Multi-track Audio

Originally, sound recording and sound reproduction were carried out using a single audio channel. In human hearing, sound received by the two ears is decoded by the brain, and the two resulting signals determine the direction of sound. This was the basis of using two audio channels [2–4] to produce *stereophonic sound*. Later, more channels were introduced to enhance the natural effects of sound. Four audio channels, for *quadraphonic sound* generation, were introduced with this consideration. Quadrophonic sound generation is also referred to as 4.0 surround sound. Currently, a more realistic sound system is produced in movie theaters and home theaters by placing one or more of the channels emitting sound behind the listeners, providing the basis for surround sound systems.

Multi-track audio recording consists of recording complex musical performances by placing microphones close to each music source (voices and instruments). To achieve a balanced recording, the microphones are connected to a mixer that can individually monitor the output of each microphone. This output can be recorded on a multi-track tape for future editing.

The size of digital audio can be calculated as follows:

Mono = sampling rate * duration of recording in seconds * (bit resolution/8) * 1 as there is 1 channel

Stereo = sampling rate * duration of recording in seconds * (bit resolution/8) * 2 as there are 2 channels

Example: For an audio CD (capacity 0.7 gigabytes) playing a song for 2.3 minutes, with a sampling rate of 44.1 kHz and bit resolution of 16 bits, what is the size?

Answer: $44100 \times 2.3 \times 60 \times 16/8 \times 2 = 24.2$ Mbytes

3.10 Psychoacoustic Model

Psychoacoustics [2–4] is the study of how sounds are perceived by humans. This is based on the concept of perceptual coding, which is a process that eliminates information from audio signals that are inaudible to the ear. This model also detects conditions under which different audio components mask (Figure 3.9) each other. This signal masking can be carried out by any of the three methods listed below:

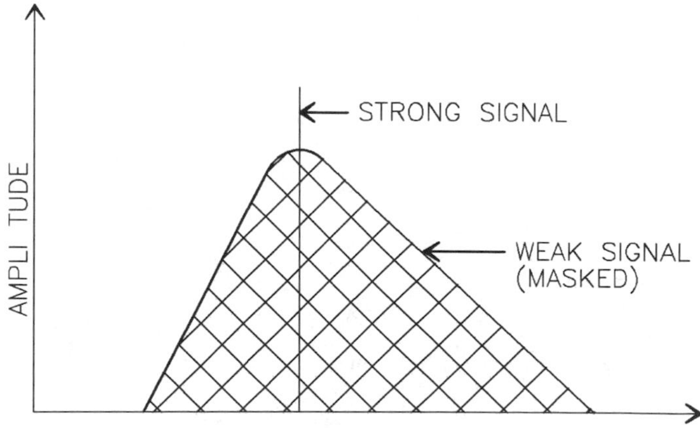

FIGURE 3.9
Audio noise masking.

- *Threshold cut-off:* Occurring in the frequency domain, where all frequencies below the threshold of human hearing are cut off.
- *Spectral masking:* Also in the frequency domain, where a frequency component can be masked fully or partially by another frequency component close to it.
- *Temporal masking:* Occurs in the time domain, when a quieter component is masked by a louder component that is temporally close to it.

3.11 Digital Audio Compression

Digital audio compression [2–4] is the process of removing redundant or otherwise irrelevant information from audio signals with the help of audio compression algorithms, which are often referred to as audio encoders. Three redundancies can occur:

- Statistical redundancy occurs when the audio samples do not have equal probability of occurrence.
- Temporal redundancy occurs when there is a strong correlation between neighboring audio signals.
- Knowledge redundancy can occur when the signal is limited in scope so that a common knowledge can be associated with both the encoder and decoder.

The advantages of compression are:

- Reduction of required storage space
- Reduction of required transmission bandwidth

The motivations for compression are:

- Streaming of data
- Interactive multimedia applications
- Efficient storage

The goals of compression are:

- To make a decoded signal sound as close as possible to the original signal
- To have the lowest implementation complexity
- To ensure that the technique(s) are robust

- To reduce the bandwidth
- To achieve scalability

Some of the commonly used compression techniques are:

- Differential pulse code modulation (DPCM)
- MPEG
- Linear predictive coding
- Mu-law compression
- Voc file compression

Compression of sound signals are required because audio consumes a substantial amount of bandwidth. Compression is achieved through the removal of redundant information using coding techniques. If the information is permanently removed and cannot be retrieved when the compressed data is uncompressed, the compression is termed lossy; otherwise, the compression technique is termed lossless. Lossy compression of audio signals occurs when the coding techniques employ the psychoacoustic model described in the previous section. MPEG is a popular lossy compression technique based on the psychoacoustic model, which is described in the next section.

The human auditory system cannot perceive all auditory signals in terms of perceived loudness and/or audibility of a test frequency. In psychoacoustics, critical bands describe the frequency bandwidths of the auditory filters created by the cochlea, the sense organ of hearing located within the inner ear. This is a band of frequencies within which a second tone interferes with the perception of the first tone, by auditory masking.

The auditory frequency analysis mechanism is unable to resolve inputs whose frequency difference is less than the critical bandwidths.

An encoder uses a bank of filters to first analyze the spectral components of the input signal from frequency transforms of a window of signal values. Subsequently, the bank of filters decomposes the signal into sub-bands.

3.11.1 MPEG

MPEG audio compression: [2–4] is a compression algorithm that uses the psychoacoustic model and thus exploits the perceptual properties of the human ear. MPEG offers sampling rates of 32, 44.1, and 48 kHz. No assumption about the nature of the audio source is required. There are three independent layers of MPEG: MPEG-1, 2, and 4.

MPEG-1 is based on the psychoacoustic model and used for digital compact cassette (DCC). The encoder can compress both mono and stereo audio signals. MPEG-2 defines two audio compression standards: MPEG-2 BC (backward compatible) is an extension of MPEG-1 that includes multichannel coding, and sampling frequencies of under 32 kHz are allowed.

MPEG-2 AAC (advanced audio coding) is a more advanced version of MPEG-2 with superior performance. MPEG-2 can be used for CD-I and DVDs. MPEG-4 audio codec can compress both natural (speech, music) and synthesized sound using structural descriptions.

Some high-fidelity multichannel audio codecs developed by Dolby Laboratories are the AC family of audio coders. There are three codecs in this family: AC-1, AC-2, and AC-3. AC-3 is widely used for high-definition TV (HDTV) and DVD.

3.11.1.1 Audio versus Speech Compression Techniques

A human vocal tract model speech compression is used to compress signals. However, due to larger number of possible signal variations, audio compression does not use this technique.

The evolution of MPEG is listed below:

MPEG-1: Used in video CD and MP3

MPEG-2: Used in digital television set-top boxes and DVD

MPEG-4: Used in fixed and mobile web

MPEG-7: Used for the description and search of audio and visual content

MPEG-21: To be used for multimedia framework

3.11.1.2 MP3

MPEG audio breaks up the input signal into its frequency components by first applying a filter bank. It also applies a psychoacoustic model in parallel to the data, and this model is used in a bit-allocation block. The number of bits allocated is used to quantize information from the filter bank. The quantization provides the compression, and bits are allocated where most needed to lower quantization noise below the audible level.

MP3 is a popular audio compression standard. Here, MP stands for MPEG-1 and 3 stands for layer 3. Layers 1–3 are audio compatible because they all include the same header information. The compression is lossy because they use the psychoacoustic model. The three layers are downward compatible, with layer 3 being the most complex and consequently having the best compression for a given audio quality.

Codecs are devices or programs for compressing and decompressing data. Layers 1 and 2 codecs use a quadrature mirror filter bank, which is a filter bank that divides the signal into two components (low frequency and high frequency). Layer 3 uses direct cosine transform (DCT). The Fourier transform (FT) is used for the psychoacoustic model.

Layer 1 of MP3 uses the psychoacoustic model for frequency masking only. It has bit rates of 32 kbps for mono and 448 kbps for stereo. Near CD stereo quality is possible with bit rates of 256–384 kbps. Layer 2 of MP3 uses the psychoacoustic model for frequency masking as well as temporal masking. It has bit rates of 32–192 kbps for mono and 64–384 kbps for stereo. Near CD stereo quality is possible with bit rates of 192–256 kbps.

Layer 3 uses a sophisticated sub-band analysis as well as non-uniform quantization and entropy coding. Bit rates are between 32 and 320 kbps.

In the auditory model, critical bands are divided into 25 segments. However, MP3 uses 32 overlapping sub-bands of uniform width. Each of the sub-bands covers several critical bands in the lower frequency range, as the width of a typical critical band is less than 100 Hz. At higher frequencies, the width of the critical band is greater than 4 kHz. For each frequency level, the sound level above masking level decides how many bits must be assigned to code signal values, so quantization noise is kept below masking level and cannot be heard.

CD audio is sampled at 44.1 kHz and 16 bits per channel, so two channels need a bit rate of 1.4 Mbps. MPEG-1 uses, on average, 256 kbps for audio. MP3 CD holds six times more audio data than the conventional CD.

MP4 or M4A is the successor to MP3. It can be imported to MP3 using an MP3 encoder. MP4 can store audio, video, still images, subtitles, and text. While converting from MP4 to MP3, only the audio portion can be converted.

To get lossless music, the free lossless audio codec (FLAC) is recommended.

Audio MP3 files as well as MP4 files are large files, so file sharing on the Internet can be done using several options, for example, using a virtual private network (VPN) or a cross-platform program like 7-Zip or file transfer protocol (FTP).

3.12 Audio File Formats

File formats provide a template in which to store audio data, along with information like sampling rates, file size, and so on. Several audio file formats and their properties are listed below:

- *m-law(.au/.snd)* is the most frequently used format on the Internet. It is small and has a player on almost all platforms. Sampled at 8 kHz. Used on Sun and NeXT platforms.
- *Audio interchange file format (.aif/.aiff/.aifc)* allows for storage of multichannel sampled sound at a variety of sample rates. Interchange format can easily be converted to other formats used in high-end audio where storage space is not a problem. Platforms include Mac and Silicon Graphics.

- *Resource interleave file format (RIFF) wave(.wav)* is like AIFF. Also requires approximately 10 Mb/min for 16-bit sampling rate of 44 kHz. Used on Microsoft and IBM platforms.
- *Motion Picture Experts Group (MPEG) (.mpg/.mp2/.mp3)* is the most popular, defined by ISO's MPEG. Uses psychoacoustic models. Supports layers and compression techniques. Layer 1 takes least amount of time, while layer 3 takes the most time to compress. All platforms.
- *Creative voice (.voc) recorded by Creative Lab's Sound Blaster (/Pro)* supports eight-bit mono audio files. All platforms.
- *Musical instrument digital interface (MIDI) (.mid/. midi)* is not a specification for sampled audio data but a serial communication protocol designed to allow transmission of control data between electronic musical instruments. All platforms.
- *AD Lib(.smp)* is used by AD Lib gold card.
- *Dialogic (.vox)* is four-bit mono, a musical DPCM format.

The last two standards are used for games and on DOS and Windows platforms.

3.13 Audio in Mobile Devices

To experience high fidelity (hi-fi) audio on mobile devices, the following requirements should be met [12]:

1. Wireless headsets should be used as headphones, with necessary hardware.
2. DAC converter. Usually dedicated DAC converters are large and often larger than the size of the smartphone. High-end mobile devices often have the necessary support to bypass its inbuilt audio output by using the charging port, like a micro-USB lightning port.
    - DACs the size of a flash drive that are low powered enough to obviate the use of a battery are available in the market.
    - The best portable DACs have built-in power supplies, volume switches, and gain settings for sound amplification.
    - Dedicated DACs often use a mini-USB port for which a micro-USB or a lightning mini-USB cable is needed.
    - Mobiles must support audio-out via a micro-USB on-the-go (OTG).

- High-end Android devices and recent models of iPhone and Window machines allow audio-out natively.
- High-end devices also have provisions for portable amplifiers in addition to portable DACs. Generally, DACs have built-in amplifiers.

  In the Bluetooth audio setup, music is transferred wirelessly, and so the DAC is built into the headset. The need for a separate DAC is obviated as the headset with built-in DAC receives the transmission and subsequently transcribes the signal into wireless sound, all within the headphone.

3. Hi-fi (or detailed) music files. DACs alone might be inadequate to provide accurate information regarding the 1s and 0s of the signal. There are two options to overcome this limitation:
   a. The first is to find uncompressed resource files.
   b. The second is to stream the signal from TIDAL, a company that allows hi-fi streaming. This will provide free lossless audio content (FLAC).

CDs can deliver 16-bit 44.1 kHz, while lossless audio can reach up to 24-bit 192 kHz. However, the lossless library consumes a lot of memory space, as expected. The maximum stream allowed is 320 kilobits per second (kbps). Lossless detail requires four times more data.

TIDAL gives FLAC sent at the rate of 1411 kbps but only at a CD quality signal rate (16-bit/44.1 kHz).

Both iPhones and Android phones come with mobile recording apps for recording music.

Review

At the end of this chapter you will have learned about the following topics:

The physical properties of audio signals, like amplitude, frequency, intensity (loudness), and audio envelopes

The two-step digitization process of converting analog audio signals to digitized audio signal

Fourier analysis of audio signals and use of sub-band signals to group different frequency bands of audio signals

Basics of music and speech recognition and synthesis

Stereophonic and quadraphonic sound

Musical instrument digital interface (MIDI)

Digital audio compression and MPEG
Psychoacoustic model
Audio file format
Audio on mobile devices

Review Questions

1. Define the terms *amplitude, frequency, intensity,* and *envelope* in relation to an audio signal.
2. Describe how an audio signal is quantized.
3. How is the Fourier analysis of an audio signal performed?
4. What is sub-band coding?
5. Define the terms *loudness, pitch,* and *timbre* in the context of music.
6. Describe the basics of staff notation in Western music.
7. How is speech recognition and synthesis done?
8. What is meant by stereophonic and quadraphonic sound?
9. What is MIDI?
10. Describe the basics of audio compression. What is MPEG?
11. What is the psychoacoustic model?
12. List some popular audio file formats, their uses, and the platforms where they can be implemented.
13. How is audio played on mobile devices?

Multiple Choice Questions

1. For audio signals, loudness is proportional to the square of:
   (a) Amplitude
   (b) Frequency
   (c) Waveform
   (d) None of the above
2. According to the Nyquist criterion, the sampling size should be
   (a) Half the frequency
   (b) Double the frequency
   (c) The square of the amplitude

   (d) The square root of the amplitude
   (e) None of the above
3. Sampling size refers to
   (a) The number of samples per second
   (b) The number of bytes per sample
   (c) The number of bits per sample
   (d) None of the above
4. Treble clef is also known as
   (a) B clef
   (b) D clef
   (c) F clef
   (d) G clef
   (e) None of the above
5. MIDI has
   (a) 4 channels
   (b) 16 channels
   (c) 8 channels
   (d) 32 channels
   (e) 2 channels
6. Speech synthesis uses which of the following for representing audio signals?
   (a) The parametric method
   (b) The waveform method
   (c) a and b
   (d) None of the above
7. For an audio CD playing a song for 1 minute on a stereo system with 16 bits and a sampling rate of 32 kHz, the size is
   (a) 5 Mbytes
   (b) 10 Mbytes
   (c) 15 Mbytes
   (d) 20 Mbytes
   (e) None of the above
8. Which cut-off occurs in the frequency domain?
   (a) Temporal masking occurs in the frequency domain
   (b) Spectral masking occurs in the time domain
   (c) All of the above

9. MPEG audio compression offers sampling rates of
   (a) 32 kHz
   (b) 44.1 kHz
   (c) 48 kHz
   (d) None of the above
   (e) All of the above
10. Which of the following is true for .riff files?
   (a) They are like .aiff
   (b) They have 16-bit resolution
   (c) Their sampling rate is 44.1 kHz
   (d) All of the above
   (e) None of the above

References

1. Prabhat K. Andleigh and Kiran Thakrar, *Multimedia Systems Design*, Upper Saddle River, NJ: Pearson Education, 1996.
2. Ralf Steinmetz and Klara Nahrstedt, *Multimedia: Computing, Communications and Applications*, Upper Saddle River, NJ: Pearson Education, 1995.
3. Ze-Nian Li and Mark S. Drew, *Fundamentals of Multimedia*, Upper Saddle River, NJ: Pearson Education, 2004.
4. Mrinal K. Mandal, *Multimedia Signals and Systems*, Boston, MA: Kluwer Academic Publishers now part of Springer Science + Business Media, 2003.
5. Fred Halsall, *Multimedia Communications: Applications, Networks, Protocols and Standards*, Upper Saddle River, NJ: Pearson Education, India, 2001.
6. Zhioua, http://faculty.kfupm.ed.sa/ICS/lahouri/.../StNotes03a.ppt, accessed 2004.
7. USUP State Faculty Lecture notes, http://faculty.uscupstate.edu/.../DigitalAudio_Chapter12.ppt (accessed August 2011).
8. Howmusicworks.org, www.howmusicworks.org/204/The-Major_Scale/Staff-Line_Notation (accessed July 2018).
9. Chris Chafe, A short history of digital sound synthesis by composers in the U.S.A. https://ccrma.stanford.edu/~cc/pub/pdf/histSynUSA.pdf (accessed August 2018).
10. Wolfgang Effelsberg, Music in Multimedia Systems, 1998. https://www.computer.org/csdl/mags/mu/1998/03/u3016.pdf (accessed September 2018).
11. The MIDI Manufacturers Association, Tutorial: MIDI and Music Synthesis, 1995, https://www.midi.org/articles-old/tutorial-midi-and-music-synthesis-1 (accessed October 2018).
12. Stefan Baumgartner, HTML5 Audio on mobile devices, 2012, https://fettblog.eu/blog/2012/04/08/html5-audio-on-mobile-devices (accessed October 2018).

4

Image in Multimedia

4.1 Introduction

An image is a spatial representation of an object or a two-dimensional (2D) or three-dimensional (3D) scene. A picture, which is a representation of a momentary event from a 3D spatial world, is an example of a 2D image, whereas a computer game can be a sequence of 3D images [1–7]. An image is modeled as a continuous function defining a rectangular region in a plane. Images formed from actual convergence of light rays are real images, whereas images formed from the extrapolation of light rays that are non-existent are imaginary. The image intensity distribution is proportional to the radiant energy received in the electromagnetic band to which the sensor/detector is sensitive (sometimes referred to as the intensity image) [1,2,6]. A digital image is represented by a matrix of numeric values, each representing a quantized intensity value I (r, c), where r is the row and c is the column. An image can be obtained in digital form by sampling the image intensity function at discrete intervals. The sample points representing the smallest discrete intensity value is called a *pixel*. A pixel [1–6] is essentially a picture element (pel) in two dimensions. A voxel is a 3D picture element of a very thin slice, or a volume element. This process of selecting the discrete points is referred to as *sampling*. The value of the intensity at each pixel is obtained by approximating the continuous value to a bin value. This approximation is referred to as *quantization*, and the approximation corresponds to the number of bits per pixel required to obtain this intensity value.

The different image representations [1,2,6] are:

1. *Black and white, or bitonic, image*: Image that corresponds to a single-color plane with two bits.
2. *Gray-scale image*: Image that has a single-color plane, typically with eight bits.
3. *Color image*: Image with three color planes, each plane typically with eight bits. Each of these planes corresponds to the primary colors red (R), blue (B), and green (G).

4. *Indexed color image*: Image that corresponds to a single-color plane that indexes a color table.
5. Images compressed according to a certain format, for example JPG, TIFF, and so on.

Color images correspond to three image planes R, G, and B, each with eight bits per pixel, resulting in a 24-bit per pixel color image. The 24-bit image representation [1] and the three-color planes are depicted in Figure 4.1.

The 24 bits associated with each pixel in the frame buffer are split into three eight-bit groups that are fed to digital to analog (DAC) converters into their analog counterparts to be displayed on the screen.

Image characteristics include intensity, color, and texture. An image histogram gives the graphical representation of the tonal distribution of a digital image. It is essentially a plot of the number of pixels for each gray level (or tonal) value. A color histogram is a composite of three such plots, one each for each primary color. Texture is the small surface structure of the image, which can be either natural or artificial, regular or irregular. Attributes ascribed to texture are regularity, coarseness, orientation, contrast, and so on.

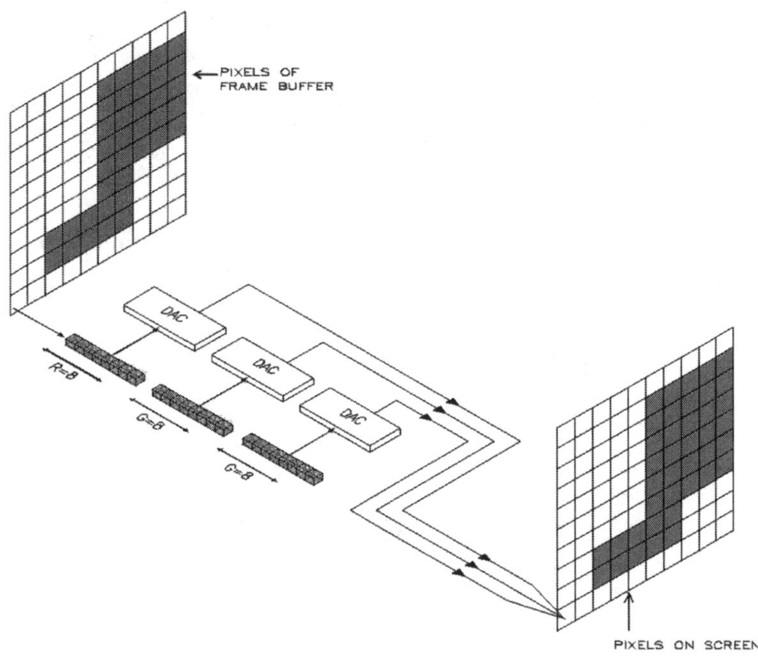

FIGURE 4.1
Graphical representation of 24-bit true color.

Image attributes can be described in the spatial domain or frequency domain. *Spatial domain* refers to the plane of intensity values, whereas *frequency domain* is a planar representation of the Fourier transform of the changing intensity values.

4.1.1 Bitmap and Vector Graphics

There are two categories of digital images storage scheme: bitmap and vector graphics [1,2,8].

Bitmap (also known as *raster scan*) images (or paint graphics) are images represented as a matrix of individual dots (or pixels) that have their own color, described using bits. Bitmap images can be divided into four categories: (1) line art images, which are bitonic, (2) gray-scale images that normally use eight bits/pixel for describing the gray scale intensity; (3) multi-tonal images, which contain two or more colors; and (4) full-color images. Image-processing applications on bitmap images can be performed with commercial software like Adobe Photoshop. Image processing is pixel-oriented in this category. A disadvantage of bitmap images is the large file size involved in storing the image. Images are captured with a digital camera or scanner that produces continuous tone and thus are of photographic quality. The resolution is defined as the number of pixels per inch (ppi). The ppi quality improves up to a maximum of 300 ppi; the minimum is 200 ppi. However, some of the disadvantages include the non-scalability of images and resolution dependence. Bitmap images are limited to rectangular shapes with a transparent, inherent background in native file formats like GIF and PNG.

Dithering is a process that produces a distinct dotted pattern approximating the color of the raster scan. This process results in the loss of fine detail and sharpness in the image, but it is useful as an approximation, when a certain color is not available, or the color monitor used to display the image is not equipped to handle the desired color.

Vector graphics are images (or plain drawn graphics) that are a collection of points (nodes), lines, and curves that produce objects. Each node, line, or curve is obtained from mathematical computations and has attributes that are editable like color, fill, and outline. Processing for this category is essentially object-oriented. Images files are small, and images are scalable without much loss of image quality. However, these images are not very accurate in detail and hence are not photorealistic. Adobe Illustrator, AutoCad, and CorelDraw are examples of commercial software packages that are used to create vector graphics images. Computer aided design (CAD) is a practical application of vector graphics.

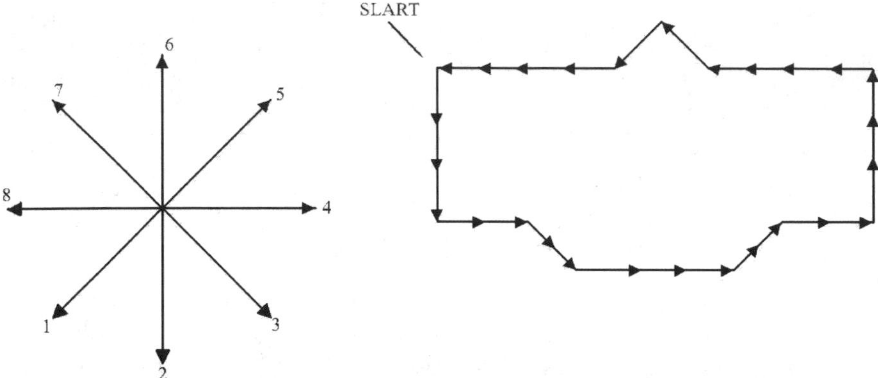

FIGURE 4.2
An example of an eight-directional chain code.

To summarize, bitmap images are used for photographs, while vector graphics are used for logos and text. Some file formats like TIFF and JPEG are only bitmap types, while EPS, PS, and PDF can be both file types. Vector graphics can easily be converted to bitmap, but converting from bitmap to vector graphics is difficult. Both bitmap and vector graphics can be incorporated into one program producing one image output using software like Adobe InDesign.

4.1.2 Image Representations

Although images are generally represented as matrices of pixel intensity values, alternate representations like chain codes [6] are also possible. Chain codes are computer algorithms for describing the shape and size of an object using direction points. The eight directional chain code, with an example representing a boundary, is shown in Figure 4.2.

4.2 Image Enhancement

Image enhancement refers to image-processing operations performed to improve the image quality according to the requirement of an application [6]. These operations can be performed on the intensity images themselves, which constitutes image enhancement in the spatial domain, or on the Fourier transforms of the intensity images, which constitutes image enhancements in the frequency domain. Image enhancement can be performed directly on the pixels, referred to as point-processing techniques, like image negation, log and power law transformations, or it is a result of neighborhood operations with the help of filters. Such filter operations include blurring, or noise removal and sharpening.

4.3 Image Segmentation

Segmentation [6] is the process of partitioning a digital image into multiple segments that are more meaningful and therefore easier to analyze. For intensity images, four popular approaches are threshold techniques, edge-based methods, region-based techniques, and connectivity-preserving relaxation methods.

Threshold techniques, which are the easiest of the segmentation techniques, make decisions based on local pixel information. They are useful when the intensity levels of the objects fall squarely outside the range of levels in the background. Because spatial information is ignored, however, blurred region boundaries cannot be properly separated.

Edge-based methods are based on discontinuities in intensity values of the pixel. Boundaries or contours of the object are detected. However, when the contours are broken, as in the case of blurred images, edges cannot be precisely defined.

Region-based techniques hinge on the continuity of intensity values of neighboring pixels. Here, the image is partitioned into connected regions by grouping neighboring pixels of similar intensity levels. Adjacent regions are then merged under some criterion involving perhaps homogeneity or sharpness of region boundaries. If the criteria are too stringent, fragmentation can result. Lenient criteria overlook blurred boundaries and thus there is often a merging of different regions. Hybrid techniques using a mix of the methods above are also popular. Figure 4.3 shows an image of a flower with leaves (center) as well as the threshold (left) and edge segmented (right) image using the Canny edge segmentation operator.

A connectivity-preserving, relaxation-based segmentation method, usually referred to as the active contour model [9], has been proposed. The proposed technique starts with some initial boundary shape represented in the form of spline curves, and it is iteratively modified by applying various shrink

FIGURE 4.3
Image and threshold and edge segmented image.

and expansion operations according to some energy function. Although the concept of energy minimization is not new, coupling it with the maintenance of an elastic contour model gives it an interesting new twist. As usual with such methods, getting trapped into a local minimum is a risk against which one must guard, and this is no easy task.

Other recent techniques include graph-based methods, watershed transformations, histogram, and compression-based methods.

4.4 Color Models

Color models [1,2,6] or color spaces refer to a color coordinate system in which each point represents one color. These models are standardized for different purposes. Three of the most important models for images are:

- Red, green, and blue (RGB) for color monitors of cathode ray tubes (CRTs) in earlier television models, liquid crystal displays (LCDs), and video cameras.
- Cyan, magenta, yellow, and black (CMYK) for color printers.
- Hue saturation intensity (HSI), which is closest to the human visual system.

The first two are hardware-based models. The third is a color manipulation model that can decouple color (or chrominance part) from the gray-scale component.

The primary colors are red (R), blue (B), and green (G). White is an addition of all three colors, that is:

$$R + G + B = W(\text{hite})$$
$$R + G = Y(\text{ellow})$$
$$R + B = M(\text{agenta})$$
$$G + B = C(\text{yan})$$

Colors formed by the mixing of primary colors are referred to as the additive color model.

The colors yellow (Y), cyan (C), and magenta (M), which are formed from the primary colors R, G, and B, are called secondary colors:

$$Y + C = G$$
$$Y + M = R$$
$$M + C = B$$
$$Y + C + M = B(\text{lack})$$

Colors formed by mixing secondary colors are referred to as the subtractive color model.

4.4.1 RGB Model

The RGB color model is an additive color model used for CRT displays: Color information can be stored directly in RGB form. The RGB model is based on the three primary colors of red, green, and blue, which together add up to white, hence the name *additive*. This coordinate system is device-dependent. When two light beams impinge on a target image, the colors add. When two phosphors in a CRT screen are turned on, their colors add; that is, red phosphor + green phosphor produces yellow light. The RGB and CMY coordinate systems are shown in Figure 4.5.

4.4.2 CMYK Model

The CMYK model, a subtractive model, is used for printing on paper (usually white paper). Yellow ink subtracts blue from white illumination but reflects red and green, which is why it appears yellow. The subtractive primary colors are cyan, magenta, and yellow. In the additive (RGB) model, there is no light at the origin (0, 0, 0).

In the subtractive model (CMY), black is obtained by subtracting all light by laying down ink with C = M = Y = 1. CMY is supposed to mix to black, but in reality it mixes to muddy black. Truly "black" ink is cheaper than mixing color inks to make black. A simpler approach to produce sharper printed images is to use colors.

Calculating that part of the three-color mix that would make black, then removing it from color proportions and adding it back as real black is a process known as *under color removal*. In the new four-dimensional (4D) space, the four coordinates are defined as follows: K = min, that is, C, M, Y; C = (C – K); M = (M – K); Y = (Y – K).

The RGB and CMY coordinate systems are depicted in Figure 4.4.

$$\begin{bmatrix} C \\ M \\ Y \end{bmatrix} = \begin{bmatrix} 1 \\ 1 \\ 1 \end{bmatrix} - \begin{bmatrix} R \\ G \\ B \end{bmatrix}$$

$$\begin{bmatrix} R \\ G \\ B \end{bmatrix} = \begin{bmatrix} 1 \\ 1 \\ 1 \end{bmatrix} - \begin{bmatrix} C \\ M \\ Y \end{bmatrix}$$

The conversion between RGB and CMY colors are given above.

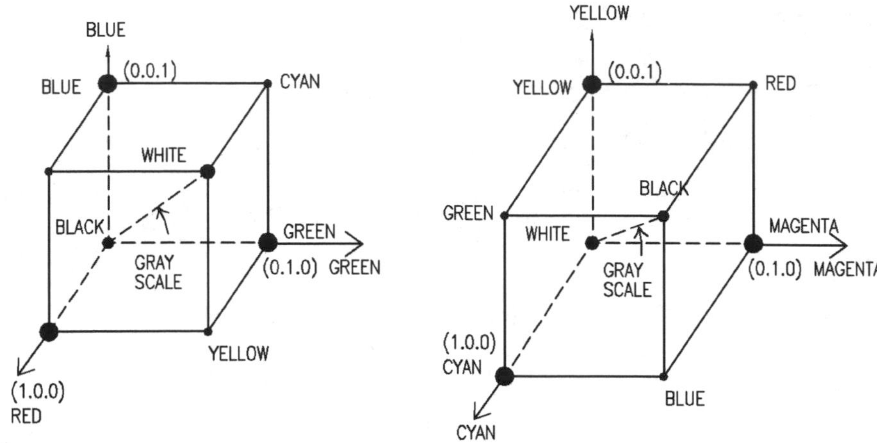

FIGURE 4.4
RGB and CMY coordinate system.

4.4.3 HSI Model

The HSI color model is also known as the hue, saturation, value (HSV) color model; it is shown in Figure 4.5. This color model is most suitable for human interpretation because it decouples the intensity component (also known as the achromatic component) from color carrying information (hue and saturation, also known as the chromatic components). Saturation gives the strength of the color; hue is the shade/color.

4.5 Some Image File Formats

Some of the common image file formats [1–7] are described below:

PostScript: Fully fledged programming language optimized for printing graphics and text. It was introduced by Adobe in 1985. Convenient for representing images in a device-independent manner.

Graphics interchange format (GIF): developed by Compuserve Information service in 1987. Easy to write programs that decodes and displays GIF images. Original GIF had 256 colors but GIF24 uses 24-bit colors (more than 16 million colors). Disadvantage: display 24-bit color using eight-bit screen so image must be dithered.

Tagged Image File Format (TIFF): Designed by Aldus in 1987 to allow portability and hardware independence for image encoding. Can save images in an almost infinite variations. It has two parts: The first part

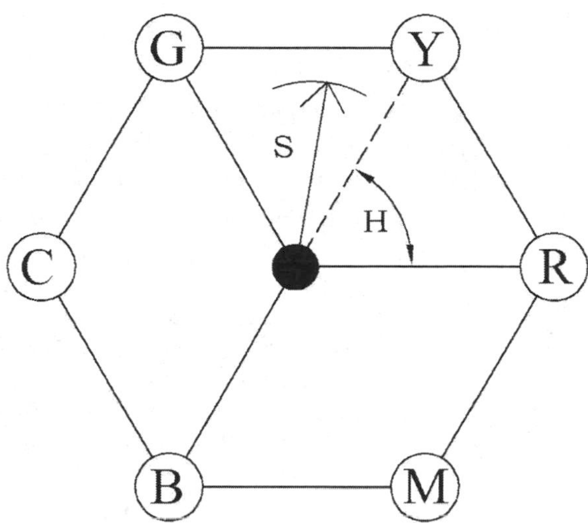

FIGURE 4.5
HSI color system.

should support display programs; the second part has extensions used to define properties, for example, the use of the CMYK color model to represent print colors.

X11 Bitmap (XBM) and X11 Pixmap (XPM): Graphic formats frequently used in UNIX to store program icons or background images. These formats allow definition of monochrome (XBM) or color (XPM) images inside programs.

Portable bitmap plus (PBMplus): Software package that allows the conversion of images between various image formats and their script-based modification. Four different image formats include:

Portable bitmap (PBM): binary images

Portable graymap (PGM): gray value images

Portable pixmap (PPM): true color images

Portable anymap (PNM) for format-independent manipulation of images

Bitmap (BMP) has the following characteristics:

Device-independent bitmap files mostly used in Windows

Uses RGB color model

Does not compress the original image

Format defines header (information about size, color depth, color table, and compression method)

Data contain the value of each pixel in a line

4.6 Images in Mobile Devices

Since cameras are an integral part of modern-day mobile devices, image processing is an important consideration in the development of these devices [10,11]. Low-end mobile devices have a very basic sensor with a low resolution that can perform only very basic image-processing tasks and color effects.

High-end mobile devices, on the other hand, have high-resolution cameras and powerful sensors that can process large images instantly using on-chip image signal processors (ISPs) and digital signal processors (DSPs). These help the mobile device in performing computationally intensive operations to produce image effects like edge detection, smoothening, filtering, embossing, and pencil sketch, to name a few, in real time, with the help of high-speed CPUs.

Image processing on mobile devices generally involves the convolving of the given image matrix, which includes the image pixels, with a predetermined matrix called the function matrix. This function matrix is usually 3 × 3 or 9 × 9 pixels, and it essentially performs filtering operations to obtain the desired effects on the image matrix. For edge detection, for instance, the function matrix is an edge detection operator like Prewitt, Roberts, or Sobel, log or zero cross. The disadvantage of this method is that it can only modify the image in a predetermined format. If multiple effects are desired, then processing becomes prohibitively computationally intensive; thus research efforts are in progress to reduce the time as well as computation on the mobile device. One way to do this is to compare the sample input and output image matrices and train the system to generate a function matrix by adaptive processing. This matrix is made to operate on the image matrix to produce the desired output. Another way is to send the image files to a central server that processes the images and sends them back. However, large images cause significant delays, resulting in added costs for data usage.

A method suggested by Durand's group at the Massachusetts Institute of Technology (MIT) [11] involves the sending of low-quality JPEG images to the server, where high-frequency noise is introduced to increase the resolution. Then image processing is performed on the sub-images obtained by breaking the images into chunks. After performing the desired operations based on a few basic parameters like luminance and brightness, which are merely numbers, the numbers are sent back to the mobile, which in turn modifies the local copy of the high-resolution image through a filtering process. Thus, bandwidth consumption is very low, and time and energy consumption are reduced substantially, in contrast to sending and receiving high-resolution images to the server.

Review

At the end of this chapter you will have learned about the following topics:

Description of a digital image
How digital images can be represented, enhanced, and segmented
The image color models, which include RGB, CMY(K), and HSI
Image file formats

Review Questions

1. What is a digital image? How can an analog image be converted into a digital image?
2. What are the different types of image representations?
3. What is a chain code representation? Explain the different chain code representations.
4. What are two ways of describing image attributes?
5. Explain the bitmap and vector graphics image storage schemes.
6. Describe the three color models: RGB, CMYK, and HSI.
7. Name some common image file formats and their salient features.

Multiple Choice Questions

1. The smallest discrete image intensity value is called:
   (a) Pixmap
   (b) Bitmap
   (c) Pixel
   (d) None of the above
2. The process of selecting discrete points in a continuous image is called
   (a) Sampling
   (b) Quantization
   (c) Chain code representation
   (d) None of the above

3. An image histogram gives
   (a) A planar representation of the Fourier transforms of the changing intensity values
   (b) A plot of the number of pixels for each grey level
   (c) The small surface structure of the image
   (d) None of the above
4. Which of the following is *not* an image enhancement technique?
   (a) Image negation
   (b) Log transformation
   (c) Image filtering
   (d) Chain code representation
5. Which of the following image segmentation techniques is based on detection of discontinuities in image intensity values?
   (a) Region growing
   (b) Power law transformation
   (c) Edge detection
   (d) Dithering
6. The connectivity-preserving, relaxation-based segmentation method is based on
   (a) Detection of discontinuities in image intensity values
   (b) The continuity of intensity values of neighboring pixels
   (c) Energy minimization
   (d) None of these
7. Which of the following is *not true* of the RGB color model?
   (a) It is an additive model
   (b) It is used in CRT displays
   (c) It is device dependent
   (d) It is used for printing on paper
8. The CMYK model has which of the following four components?
   (a) R, G, B, and K
   (b) C, M, Y, and K
   (c) H, S, I, K
   (d) None of the above
9. The HSI model
   (a) Is additive
   (b) Is subtractive

(c) Decouples intensity component from color carrying information
(d) Is none of the above

10. Which of the following is true about the tagged image file format (TIFF)?
    I. It is portable
    II. It is device Independent
    III. It uses the CMYK color model
    IV. It uses the RGB model
        (a) I, II, III
        (b) II, III, IV
        (c) I, II, IV
        (d) None of the above

References

1. Ralf Steinmetz, Klara Nahrstedt, *Multimedia: Computing, Communications and Applications*, Upper Saddle River, NJ: Pearson Education, 1995.
2. Ze-Nian Li and Mark S. Drew, *Fundamentals of Multimedia*, Upper Saddle River, NJ: Pearson Education, 2004.
3. Mrinal K. Mandal, *Multimedia Signals and Systems*, Boston, MA: Kluwer Academic Publishers now part of Springer Science + Business Media, 2003.
4. Prabhat K. Andleigh and Kiran Thakrar, *Multimedia Systems Design*, Upper Saddle River, NJ: Pearson Education, India, 1996.
5. Fred Halsall, *Multimedia Communications: Applications, Networks*, Upper Saddle River, NJ: Protocols and Standards, Pearson Education, India, 2001.
6. Robert E. Woods and Rafael C. Gonzalez, *Digital Image Processing*, Upper Saddle River, NJ: Prentice Hall Technical Education, 1992.
7. Kay Vaughan, *Multimedia: Making It Work*, 6th edition, Berkeley CA: McGraw-Hill, 2004.
8. Colorgen limited United Kingdom, http://www.largeformatsupport.co.uk/Difference between bitmap and vector.pdf (accessed September 2018).
9. Kass, Michael, Andrew Witkin and Demetri, Terzopoulos, Snakes: Active contour models, *International Journal of computer Vision*, 1, 321–331, 1987.
10. Larry Hardesty, *Streamlining Mobile Image Processing*, Cambridge, MA: MIT News Office, November 2015. http://news.mit.edu/2015/streamlining-mobile-image-processing-1113 (accessed June 2018).
11. Michaël Gharbi, Yi Chang Shih, Gaurav Chaurasia, Jonathan Ragan-Kelley, Sylvain Paris, Frédo Durand, Transform Recipes for Efficient Cloud Photo Enhancement, Paper presented at SIGGRAPH ASIA 2015.

5

Video in Multimedia

5.1 Introduction

The process of electronically capturing, storing, transmitting, and reconstructing sequences of still images representing scenes in motion is referred to as **video technology** [1–7]. In video [1,2], a *field* is one of many still images displayed sequentially to create the impression of motion on the screen. The frame rate is the number of still pictures per unit time. Interlacing involves the alternate display of fields containing either even or odd lines only. Two fields comprise one video *frame*. Interlacing was used in the early days of standardization to reduce flicker. It would have been difficult otherwise to transmit the information in full frame quickly enough to avoid flicker. De-interlacing can be performed when the frame rate or frame size needs to be changed. One method is to discard one field and duplicate the other field's scan lines. However, information from one field is completely lost.

Video can be interlaced or progressive. **Interlaced** video is a technique of doubling the perceived frame rate introduced with the video signal used with analog television without consuming extra bandwidth. Since the interlaced signal contains two fields of a video frame shot at two different times, it enhances motion perception to the viewer and reduces flicker (a visible fading between two cycles) due to the persistence of vision effect. **Progressive** scanning is the process of displaying, storing, or transmitting moving images in which all lines of each frame are drawn in sequence.

Display resolution. The size of a video image is measure in pixels for digital video or horizontal scan lines and vertical lines of resolution for analog video. Video resolution for a three-dimensional (3D) video is measured in *voxels* (volume picture element).

Aspect ratio is defined as the ratio between the width and height of the screen. For traditional television, this is 4:3; for high-definition television (HDTV), this is 16:9.

Video quality can be measured with formal metrics like peak signal-to-noise ratio (PSNR), or it can be subjective video quality using expert observation. *Bit rate* gives the measure of the rate of information content in a video stream in the case of digital video and this provides a measure of video quality.

5.2 Video Color Models

There are generally two video color models [1,2], YUV (and the closely related YCbCr) and YIQ.

The YUV color model is based on the human visual system. Since the human visual system is more sensitive to brightness than color, a suitable encoding scheme would separate the luminance (brightness) component Y from the two chrominance (color) channels U and V. For compatibility with black and white receivers, the luminance (or Y) component must always be transmitted. The YUV signal is calculated as follows:

$$Y = 0.30 * R + 0.59 * G + 0.11 * B$$

$$U = 0.493 * (B-Y)$$

$$V = 0.877 * (R-Y)$$

YUV was originally used for PAL and SECAM TV standards but now it is also used for CCIR 601.

The YCbCr color model is a scaled and shifted version of the YUV color model with the following definitions:

$$Cb = ((B-Y)/2) + 0.5$$

$$Cr = ((R-Y)/1.6) + 0.5$$

The chrominance values of YcbCr are always in the range 0–1. YcbCr is used for JPEG and MPEG.

A typical image and its Y, U, and V components are shown in Figure 5.1. Note that the Y (luminance) component is prominent compared to the chrominance components U and V; thus, the Y component appears very similar to the original image.

For the YIQ color model, U and V are more simply defined but do not capture the most-to-least hierarchy of human sensitivity. Encoding for the YIQ color model is as follows:

$$Y = 0.30 * R + 0.59 * G + 0.11 * R$$

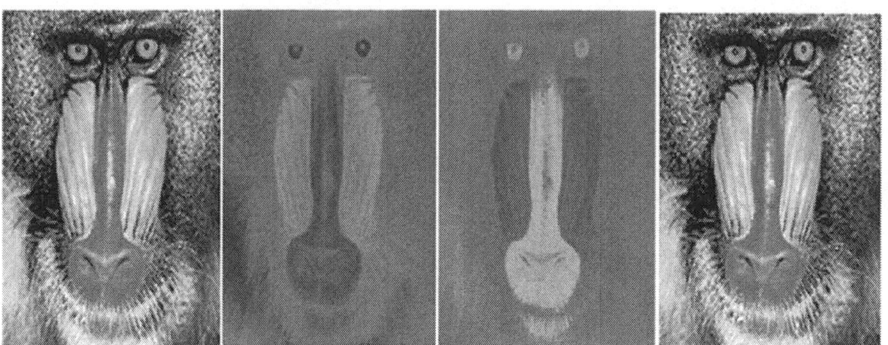

FIGURE 5.1
An image (top) and its U (second from left), V (second from right), and Y (right) components.

$$I = 0.60 * R - 0.28 * G - 0.32 * B$$

$$Q = 0.21 * R - 0.52 * G - 0.31 * B$$

I is the phase chrominance, and Q is the quadrature chrominance component. I corresponds to the axis, and Q is the purple green axis. YIQ is used with National Television Standards Committee (NTSC).

5.3 Types of Video Signals

There are three types of signals [1,2]:

1. **Component video**: The salient features are:
   - Used for higher end video systems such as studios.
   - Has three wires/connectors connecting cameras and other devices to TV/monitor.
   - Color signals not restricted to RGB but can also be YUV or YIQ.
   - Requires higher bandwidth.
   - Requires good synchronization of the three components.
   - No crosstalk between the three different channels.
2. **S-video (separated video or super video)**: The salient features are:
   - Two wires used, one for chrominance and one for luminance.
   - Crosstalk between color components and intensity component is avoided.
   - The reason for luminance being in a separate wire is because black and white information is very important for visual perception.

3. **Composite video**: The salient features are:
   - Signals (luminance and chrominance) are mixed into a single carrier wave, with the chroma signal at the higher frequency end of the channel shared with luminance.
   - There is some amount of interference between the signals.
   - Chrominance and luminance are separated at the receiver end.

5.4 Analog Video

Smooth analog signals match recorded sound better than stepwise digital recording. However, analog media, like vinyl or magnetized tape on which the signals are recorded, can have imperfections resulting in cracking and popping noise. Furthermore, digital signals maintain the quality of signals, even over long distances. Digital video content carries more information than their analog counterparts, whether optical fibers, cables, or radio waves are used as carriers. Nevertheless, analog signals are still very important in the video context for better understanding video performance.

There are two types of analog video: progressive and interlaced. As mentioned earlier, progressive scanning traces through the complete picture (frame) row-wise for each time interval, whereas in interlaced scanning, odd numbered lines are traced first and then even number lines are traced. Thus, interlaced scanning consists of two fields per frame: one corresponding to the odd lines and the other corresponding to the even lines. The scan lines are not perfectly horizontal because a small voltage is applied moving the electron beam downward over time. Odd lines end in the middle of the line and even lines start from the middle. Interlacing was invented to avoid flicker. However, it is difficult to transmit information in the full frame quickly enough to avoid flicker. Figure 5.2 is a schematic of a typical interleaved scan. Odd and even fields as well as horizontal and vertical retrace are shown in the figure.

The voltage applied to the cathode ray tube (CRT) used in older TV sets is a one-dimensional time varying signal. By applying a small negative value like 0.5 V to the CRT to indicate black and another value, such as zero, the start of a new line is determined, as shown in Figure 5.3.

5.4.1 Analog Video Standards

There are three major standards for color encoding in analog television systems: National Television Standards Committee (NTSC), phase alternating line (PAL), and sequential couleur avec memoire (SECAM) [1,2]. All three have an aspect ratio of 4:3. Other salient features are described below.

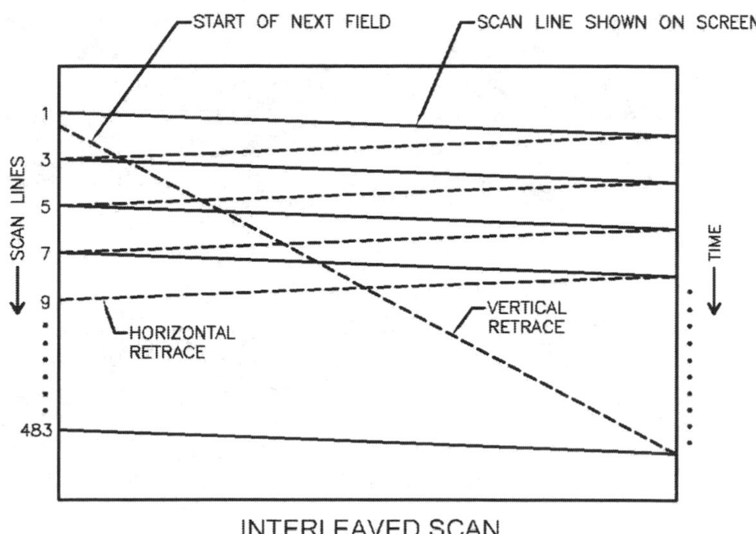

FIGURE 5.2
Interleaved scan.

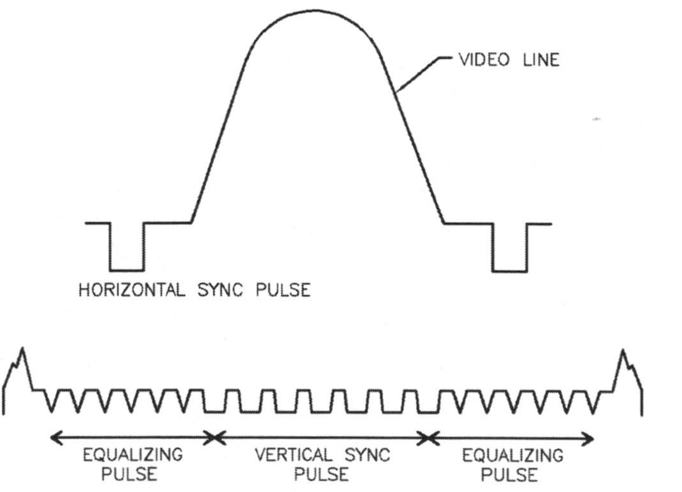

FIGURE 5.3
Voltage offset to show new line.

NTSC

This standard is widely used in North America and Japan. It uses the interlaced scan system with 525 scan lines/sec and with 29.97 frames per sec. For vertical retrace and sync, the blanking information is placed in 20 lines at the beginning of each field, so there are 485 active video lines. For horizontal blanking and retrace, 1/6 of the raster at the left side is blanked. The non-blanking pixels are referred to as active pixels. Here the YIQ color model is used. The total channel width is 6.0 MHz, with a bandwidth allocation of 4.2 MHz for Y, 1.2 MHz for I, and 0.6 MHz for Q. The system performs interlaced scanning and has a standard aspect ratio of 4:3.

PAL

PAL was originally used in Germany, but it is currently used by the United Kingdom, India, and China also. Here interlaced scanning is also used, with 625 scan lines per sec at a rate of 25 fps and standard aspect ratio. PAL uses the YUV color model. Picture quality is improved using chroma signals with alternate signs (e.g., +U or −U) in successive scan lines. PAL has better spatial resolution than NTSC, but NTSC has better temporal resolution for images. The total bandwidth allocation is 8 MHz. The bandwidth allocation is 5.5 MHz for Y, 1.8 MHz for U, and 1.8 MHz for V.

SECAM

This standard, used in France and Eastern Europe, is also based on the YUV color model. Interlaced scanning is also used, with 625 lines/sec at 25 fps. The standard aspect ratio of 4:3 is used. However, U and V signals are modulated (via frequency modulation) using separate color subcarriers and sent in alternate lines (e.g., either U or V). The total bandwidth allocation is 8 MHz. The bandwidth allocation is 6.0 MHz for Y, 2.0 MHz for U, and 2.0 MHz for V. The two main differences with the other two systems are the use of frequency modulation to encode chrominance information in the subcarrier, and the transmission of one color at a time, thus eliminating color artifacts present in the NTSC and PAL systems.

HDTV

The HDTV standard provides higher resolution than the other analog TV standards described above. The aspect ratio for HDTV is 16:9. Previously, HDTV was based on analog technology but, currently it is based on digital technology and video compression.

5.4.2 Digital Video

Digital video is replacing analog video as a method of choice for multimedia use because digital technology enables the production of finished products at a fraction of the cost and time compared to analog video. By connecting a camcorder to a computer workstation, the analog-to-digital conversion step using expensive video cards is eliminated. Also, digital video provides the scope for nonlinear video editing and production.

There are two widely used methods for video editing: the more popular bluer screen, ultimate method, which does not require expensive sets, and chromo editing.

Great backgrounds can be generated using 3D modeling and graphic software. One or more actors, vehicles, or other objects can be neatly layered onto the background.

Full integration of motion video is possible with digital gear. With a mass storage device such as a hard disk or CD-ROM, the video clip can be played back directly on a computer monitor without using any accessories. However, for playback, software architecture such as QuickTime or AVI, to name a few, is required. Video overlay is used for analog-to-digital conversion, and it is delivered using suitable hardware or directly using FireWire cables.

5.4.3 Video Capture

The process of converting an analog signal to a video signal is referred to as **video capture** [1,2]. The capture process involves several steps. Digitization converts analog signals to a raw digital data stream. Then luminance and chrominance components are then separated in composite video. (This step is not necessary for S-video.) Color difference is inducted by demodulating the chrominance component. Data is then transformed using a color space converter to generate data in any standard color model like YUV, YCbCr, or YIQ. These steps also decode data to analog video formats like NTSC or PAL.

ITU-R Recommendation BT is a standard published by the International Telecommunication Union–Radio Communications Sector for encoding interlaced analog signals into digital video form. It also includes methods of encoding 525-line 60 Hz and 625-line 50 Hz signals, both with 720 luminance samples and 360 chrominance samples per line.

5.5 Image and Video Compression Standards

For conservation of network bandwidth, one must compress image and video [1–3,6]. One of the big advantages of digital video is that it can be compressed for reduced bandwidth applications, including transmission over satellite (full-size, full-motion video requires transmission at 30 Mb per second), cable TV, and Internet-based networks. Compressed video is particularly useful for reducing storage requirements: One frame of video component at 24 bits requires 1 Mb of storage, and a 30 sec full motion clip takes up 1 Gb of hard disk space. This is especially advantageous in the broadcast and government markets.

Video compression can be lossy or lossless [1–7]. Lossless compression is particularly useful when the data needs to be reproduced in its entirety.

However, lossy compression is required for some critical broadcast or military applications when fast transmission is required, even with the loss of some relatively unimportant information. Alphanumeric data can be compressed using lossless coding techniques such as Huffman coding or Lempel-Ziv Welch (LZW) coding.

There are two parallel standards for video compression: the Moving Picture Experts Group (MPEG) and the International Telecommunication Union (ITU). These committees do not give standards for end-user product or equipment. However, MPEG does standardize profiles. A profile is a selection of tools that a group of participating companies within the standard use as a basis for deploying products to meet specific applications. For example, MPEG-4 Simple Profile (SP) and Advanced Simple Profile (ASP) were developed for streaming video over the Internet.

MPEG1 and MPEG2 are the current standards. With MPEG1, it is possible to get 1.2 Mbps of video and 250 Kbps of two-channel stereo audio using CD-ROM technology. MPEG2, a completely different system from MPEG1, requires higher data rates (3–15 Mbps) but delivers higher image resolution, better picture quality, interlaced video formats, multiresolution scalability, and multichannel audio features. Both MPEG-1 and MPEG-2 use the discrete cosine transform (DCT) algorithm to first convert each image into the frequency domain and then process the frequency coefficients to optimally reduce a video stream to the required bandwidth.

5.6 Digital File Formats

Some popular digital file formats include Audio Video Interleave (AVI) for the video container market and Windows Media Video (WMV). These formats have less compression than other file formats and therefore have more accurate image quality. Two quick formats widely used for feature-length movies are MOV and QT. These provide a diverse array of video content. For Flash, the formats are FLV, which was the original format for FLASH and shock wave flash (SWF) for Flash animation. Another file format is Advanced Video Encoding High Definition (AVCHD).

Digital video is composed of a series of orthogonal bitmap (BMP) images at rates of 15, 24, 30, and 60 fps, depending on the application required. Video can be upscaled, from low resolution to high resolution, with loss of quality, and downscaled, without loss of quality. Typical screen resolutions for surveillance (at 5 fps) and entertainment TV (at 25 fps) are 640 × 480 pixels, whereas for multimedia (at 15 fps) and video telephony (at 10 fps), the resolution is 320 × 240 pixels.

5.7 Video on Mobile Phones

Handheld devices can be used to play video through specially built apps and some mobile browsers. JISC Digital Media [8] provides help with digitizing, preserving, encoding, and hosting audiovisual files. Video codecs like HTML5 with H.264 (for MP3) and Vorbis using WebM are useful for providing video content.

Review

At the end of this chapter you will have learned about the following topics:

The basics of video technology
Video color models
Video signals
Analog video and analog video standards
HDTV and digital video
Image and video standards

Review Questions

1. Define the word *video*.
2. Explain the two types of video scanning.
3. Explain the following terms: *display resolution, aspect ratio,* and *video quality*.
4. Describe the three types of video signals.
5. Describe the important video color models.
6. What are the three important analog video standards?
7. What is HDTV?
8. What are the salient features of digital video?
9. How is video capture performed?
10. Discuss MPEG compression.

Multiple Choice Questions

1. A video is a(n)
   (a) Still image
   (b) Sound clipping
   (c) Sequence of still images
   (d) Animated image
2. A video frame is composed of
   (a) A still image
   (b) Two still images
   (c) A video field
   (d) Two video fields
3. Interlaced video
   (a) Doubles the frame rate
   (b) Halves the frame rate
   (c) Does not change the frame rate
   (d) None of the above
4. The aspect ratio for traditional television is
   (a) 1:2
   (b) 2:3
   (c) 4:3
   (d) 16:9
5. The NTSC video standard uses
   (a) 525 scan lines/sec and 30 frames per second
   (b) 525 scan lines and 25 frames per second
   (c) 625 scan lines and 30 frames per second
   (d) 625 scan lines and 30 frames per second
6. Which of the following video standards is used in India?
   (a) NTSC
   (b) PAL
   (c) SECAM
   (d) CCITT
7. In the YIQ color model
   (a) Y standards for luminance, I stands for brightness, and Q for hue
   (b) Y standards for intensity, I stands for phase chrominance, and Q stands for quadrature chrominance

 (c) Y stands for saturation, I stands for intensity, and Q stands for hue
 (d) None of the above
8. Which type of video signal is used for higher-end video signals and studio?
 (a) S video
 (b) Composite video
 (c) Component video
 (d) None of the above
9. The aspect ratio of HDTV is
 (a) 4:3
 (b) 16:9
 (c) 2:1
 (d) None of the above
10. Which of the following coding schemes is use for JPEG-2000?
 (a) Huffman coding
 (b) Arithmetic coding
 (c) LZW coding
 (d) None of the above

References

1. Ralf Steinmetz and Klara Nahrstedt, *Multimedia: Computing, Communications and Applications*, Pearson Education, 1995.
2. Ze-Nian Li and Mark S. Drew, *Fundamentals of Multimedia*, Pearson Education, 2004.
3. Mrinal K. Mandal, *Multimedia Signals and Systems*, Kluwer Academic Publishers (now part of Springer Science + Business Media), 2003.
4. Prabhat K. Andleigh and Kiran Thakrar, *Multimedia Systems Design*, Pearson Education, India, 1996.
5. Fred Halsall, *Multimedia Communications: Applications, Networks, Protocols and Standards*, Pearson Education, India, 2001.
6. Robert E. Woods and Rafael C. Gonzalez, *Digital Image Processing*, Prentice Hall Technical Education, 1992.
7. Kay Vaughan, *Multimedia: Making It Work*, McGraw-Hill, 2004.
8. JISC, Full-guide/using-digital-media-in-new-learning-models, 2015, https://www.jisc.ac.uk/full-guide/using-digital-media-in-new-learning-models2015 (accessed September 2018).

6

Animation and Computer Graphics

6.1 Introduction

Animation is to bring still objects and characters to life on a computer or mobile screen. An animation involves all changes that have a visual effect, for example, form, color, transparency, structure, and texture of an object as well as changes in lighting, camera position, orientation, and focus [1]. The combination of a biological phenomenon known as persistence of vision and a psychological phenomenon called phi, which is responsible for persistence of vision, makes animation possible. Conventional animation is created in a fairly fixed sequence consisting of a storyboard, which is an animation in outline form; a participating object, whose definition is given in terms of basic shapes such as polygons and splines; key frames, which are the frames in which the entities being animated are at extreme or characteristic positions; and finally in-between frames, which are the intermediate frames inferred from key frames [1–7]. Morphing, a process that transforms object shapes from one form to another, tweaking that deals with movement of one object over the other, and simulating accelerations that provide animation paths between key frames are procedures used in animation. A few methods are presented briefly for the specification object motion in an animation system.

Animation is widely used in industrial applications such as control system and heads-up displays, flight simulators for aircraft, and scientific research; and in the entertainment industry (examples are motion pictures, cartoons, video games), advertising, and education. The scientific applications of computer graphics and animation in scientific phenomena such as molecular bombardment is called scientific visualization. This involves the interdisciplinary fields of the application of graphics to science and engineering and other disciplines such as signal processing, computational geometry, and database theory. Often, the animations in scientific visualization are generated from simulations of scientific phenomena. The results of simulations may be large data sets representing two-dimensional (2D) or three-dimensional (3D) data (e.g., fluid flow simulations). These data are converted into images that constitute the animation. The simulation may generate positions and locations of physical objects, which must be rendered in some form to generate animation. For example, simulation of the navigation of a prototype robot manipulator in a robot workspace would give information for animation. In some cases, the simulation program contains an embedded animation language for simultaneously accomplishing both simulation and animation processes.

6.1.1 Basic Concepts of Animation

Animation involves an input comprising of key frames and then interpolating in-between processes to generate intermediate frames. Subsequently, by changing the composition of the frames thus generated, desired special effects can be obtained as described below. Changing colors is also a technique to generate animation images at a much lower bandwidth.

Input process: Drawings and photos must be digitized to key frames and then carefully post-processed (e.g., filtering) to clean up glitches arising from the input process.

In-between process: Composition of intermediate frames from key frames performed using interpolation. The simplest is linear interpolation (lerping). This is often unrealistic, so splines are used to smooth out the interpolation between key frames.

Composition stages: Individual frames in a completed animation are generated by using composition techniques to combine foreground and background elements.

Changing colors: Animation uses colour look-up table (CLUT)/look-up table (LUT), which requires only a few hundred to thousand bytes as opposed to a bandwidth of about 9 Mbits/sec to transfer about 30 images/sec.

6.1.2 Specification of Animation

Some of the common approaches in the specification of animation are listed below:

- Linear-list notation: Each event in animation is described by a beginning frame number and action (event) to be performed, for example, 42, 53, Rotate Palm, 1, 30.
- High-level programming language notation: Describes animation by embedding control in a general-purpose programming language, for example, ASAS (primitives include vectors, colors, polygons, surfaces, etc.).

- Graphical languages: In textual programming languages, graphics cannot be easily visualized, so animators use graphical languages, for example, GENESYS.

6.1.3 Display of Animation

To display with raster systems, animated objects must be scanned, converted, and stored as a pixmap in a frame buffer. Scan conversion rates around 15–20 times/sec give a reasonably smooth, visual effect. Scan conversion should take a small portion of total time; otherwise, there is a distracting ghost effect that must be corrected using double buffering.

6.1.4 Transmission of Animation

Transmission of animation is performed using two approaches:

1. Symbolic representation: Symbolic representation of animation objects is transmitted together with operations performed on the objects. In this approach, byte size is smaller than 2, but the display time is longer.
2. Pixmap representation: The transmission time is longer, but the display time is shorter.

6.1.5 Some Popular Animation Tools

Some popular animation tools include:

- 3D Max: Developed by Autodesk, 3D Max is a powerful 3D rendering, modeling, and animation tool for game developers, visual effects artists, and graphic designers. It has provisions for working with vector graphics.
- Flash: Adobe Flash Professional CS5 authoring tools create Flash projects like simple animations and video content. Flash applications are called small web format (SWF) applications and operate on the concepts of stages and layering. These applications are suitable for delivery over the Web because SWF files take very little time to download. Flash projects make extensive use of vector graphics. Graphic elements can be converted to symbols.
- Blender: Blender is an open-source 3D modeling and animation tool. Although it is packed with various functionalities, it is difficult to use. Blender also incorporates 2D and 3D vector graphics.
- AutoDesk Maya: Maya by AutoDesk Inc. is a powerful 3D modeling, visual effects, animation, and graphics tool. It can provide vector graphics as well as photorealistic images.

6.1.6 Virtual Reality

Virtual reality is a high-end user interface that involves real-time simulation and interaction through multiple sensory channels.

6.1.7 Character Animation

Character animation involves bringing animated characters to life. Two-dimensional images can be combined with 3D motion data with the help of projective cameras using pose models. The interested reader is referred to [8].

Other methods using texture in images can be used as well. Adobe has a 2D Character Animator CC for this purpose.

6.1.8 Motion Graphics

Motion graphics [9,10] are pieces of digital footage or animation that create the illusion of motion. It is an evolving art form, with sweeping camera paths and 3D elements. Maxon's CINEMA 4D, plugins such as MoGraph and Adobe's After Effects, as well as Autodesk's Maya and 3D Studio Max ae useful for motion graphics.

A particle system is a motion graphics technology that can generate animated objects using points in 2D or 3D space with a procedural animation methodology. Particles used to create the animation can be either points, lines, grids, boxes, or spheres, to name a few. This technology is popular in motion graphics.

6.1.9 Visual Effects (VFX)

Visual effects (VFX) [9,10] refers to the process of creating imagery and manipulating it outside the context of the actual filmmaking process. Categories of visual effects include animation, compositing, matte painting, modeling, simulation FX, and motion capture.

6.2 Computer Simulation

Computer simulation creates and analyzes programs that simulate the behavior of real-world systems. Computer simulation involves display building, model creation, decision making, and temporal management.

6.3 Morphing

One image can be transformed into another by morphing. It is basically an animation technique that allows users to blend two still images to create a sequence of in-between pictures that, when played in Quick Time, metamorphoses the first image into the second. The morph process consists of:

1. Warping two images so that they have the same shape
2. Cross dissolving the resulting images

6.4 Computer Graphics

Computer graphics [7] deals with all aspects of creating images on computers, namely, hardware, software, and applications. The hardware is a personal computer (PC) with a graphics card for modeling and rendering. Autodesk Maya built on top of openGL is typical software used for modeling and rendering.

Computer graphics involves the drawing of pictures on computers, a process called rendering. Such pictures can be photographs, drawings, movies, and simulations, or even pictures that cannot be seen by the eye, such as medical images. The essential processes involved in computer graphics can be stated as:

1. Imaging = representing 2D images
2. Modeling = representing 3D objects
3. Rendering = constructing 2D images from 3D models

The objective of computer graphics is the creation, storage, and manipulation of geometric objects, referred to as modeling, and the images are referred to as rendering. These images can be displayed on screens and hard-copy devices. The user should be able to control the contents, structure, and appearance of the images with the help of image-processing techniques, which include:

1. Filtering
2. Warping
3. Composition

A 3D world scene is composed of a collection of 3D models. Three different coordinate systems (or spaces) are defined for different model-related operations: object space, world space, and screen space. The coordinate system in which a specific 3D object is defined is the object space, whereas the world space is the coordinate system of the 3D world to be rendered. The screen space is the 2D space that represents the boundaries of the image to be produced. For drawing pictures on computers from photographs, drawings, and so on, a process known as scanning, described in the next section, is performed.

6.4.1 Raster Scan versus Vector Scan

Raster scan: The image produced as an array (the *raster*) of picture elements (*pixels*) in the frame buffer. Scanning is done one line at a time from top to bottom and from left to right. A video controller is required. Scans are converted to pixels. Starting from lines and wire frame images, one can get to filled polygons. Even for complex images, there is no flicker.

Vector scan: A vector scan or random scan display involves scanning between end points. This scan technique can only draw lines and characters. Scans are not converted to pixels. For complex images, flicker is present. A video controller is not required. Vector scan is costlier than raster scan.

6.4.2 Computer Graphics Applications

There are numerous applications of computer graphics, a few of which are listed below:

- Entertainment: Includes motion pictures, music videos, TV shows, and computer games.
- Computer-aided design (CAD): Includes computer-aided design for engineering and architectural systems.
- Scientific visualization: For analyzing and visualizing scientific, engineering, and medical data and behavior. Converting data to visual forms helps in understanding the significance of a large volume of data.
- Training: Specialized computer-generated models of specialized systems can assist in the training of ship captains, aircraft pilots, and so on.
- Education: Computer graphics can provide visual representations of theoretical concepts in many areas of physics and engineering (e.g., fluid dynamics, motion of particles), thus making these concepts easier to understand.

FIGURE 6.1
Example of computer graphics. (www.free.pik.com/free-photos-vectors/computer-graphics. Created by Rawpixel.com-Freepik.com.)

An example of computer graphics is shown in Figure 6.1.

6.4.3 2D Transformations

One of the most common and important tasks in computer graphics is to transform the coordinates of either objects within the graphical scene or the camera viewing the scene. Another task is to transform coordinates from one coordinate system to another (e.g., world coordinates to viewpoint coordinates, to screen coordinates). All these transformations can be performed using some simple matrix representations, which can be particularly useful for combining multiple transformations into a single composite transform matrix. This section presents simple translation, scaling, and rotation in 2D.

6.4.3.1 Translation in 2D

A point (X, Y) is to be translated by amount Dx and Dy to a new location (X′, Y′):

$$X' = Dx + X$$

$$Y' = Dy + Y$$

or

$$P' = T + P$$

6.4.3.2 Scaling in 2D

A point (X, Y) is to be scaled by amount Sx and Sy to location (X′, Y′):

$$X' = Sx * X$$

$$Y' = Sy * Y$$

or

$$P' = S * P$$

Scaling is can only be done about the **origin (0,0)**. The center of the object cannot be used for this purpose.

For upscaling, that is, scale > 1, the object is enlarged and moved away from the origin.

For scale = 1, no scaling is required.

For downscaling, that is, scale < 1, the object is shrunk and moved toward the origin.

For uniform scaling, Sx = Sy.

For differential scaling, Sx! = Sy. The proportions of the objects are altered.

6.4.3.3 Rotation in 2D

A point (X, Y) is to be rotated about the origin by angle θ to location (X′, Y′) using the transformation:

$$X' = X * \cos(\theta) - Y * \sin(\theta)$$

$$Y' = X * \sin(\theta) + Y * \cos(\theta)$$

Note that this does involve sin and cos, which are costlier than addition or multiplication or P′ = R * P, P being the original vector at (X, Y), P′ being the rotated vector (X′,Y′), and R being the rotation matrix given by

$$R = \begin{bmatrix} \cos & -\sin \\ \sin & \cos \end{bmatrix}.$$

These transformations can be extended to 3D for 3D modeling.

6.5 Rendering

Rendering is a mechanism responsible for producing a 2D image from 3D models. The important subtasks involved in rendering are:

1. Scan conversion: Deciding which pixels in the image are covered by each object
2. Visible surface algorithms: Deciding which pixels of each object are visible
3. Illumination and shading: Assigning colors to the different pixels

There are two approaches to the rendering algorithms:

1. Pixel-oriented rendering using ray tracers
2. Polygon-oriented rendering using scan-line renderers

Ray tracers operate by tracing theoretical light rays as they intersect objects in the scene and the projection plane. The limitations of ray tracers include:

1. Processor intensive. A full ray tracer is unsuitable for real-time applications.
2. Does not consider interreflections of diffuse light, resulting in hard shadows.

Scan-line renderers operate on the following principles:

1. Require all objects, including those modeled with continuous curvature, to be tessellated into polygons.
2. Operate on an object-by-object basis, directly drawing each polygon to the screen.
3. Polygons are eventually tessellated into pixels.

The illumination of scan-line renderers is performed in two steps:

1. Lighting and shading are calculated using the normal vector.
2. The color is linearly interpolated across the polygon surface.

Common shading techniques for scan-line renderers include flat shading, Gouraud shading and Phong shading.

Review

At the end of this chapter you will have learned about the following topics:

Animation: the basic processes involved
Display, control, and transmission of animation
Some popular tools in animation
Character animation, motion graphics, and visual effects
Computer simulation and morphing
Computer graphics and related applications
Raster scan versus vector (or random display) scan
Two-dimensional transformations in computer graphics
Rendering

Review Questions

1. What is animation and what are the basic steps involved?
2. How are display, control, and transmission of animation carried out?
3. Describe some popular animation tools.
4. What is computer simulation and morphing?
5. What is computer graphics and what are its applications?
6. Explain the basic 2D transformations of translation, rotation, and scaling.
7. What is computer graphics rendering?

Multiple Choice Questions

1. Animation is a ____________ multimedia object.
   (a) Temporal
   (b) Static
   (c) Dynamic
   (d) Hazy

2. For a smooth effect, scan conversion in animation must be performed at least ____________ times.
   (a) 10
   (b) 20
   (c) 30
   (d) 40
3. What is another expression for lerping?
   (a) Linear interpolation
   (b) B-spline fitting
   (c) Cubic Bezier curve fitting
   (d) Convex hull
4. Which of the following is not an animation tool?
   (a) Blender
   (b) 3Ds Max
   (c) Latex
   (d) Autodesk Maya
5. Computer graphics involves ____________ of images.
   (a) The creation
   (b) The manipulation
   (c) The storage
   (d) None of the above
   (e) All of the above
6. Which of the following is (are) true for a raster scan?
   (a) The image is produced as an array of pixels
   (b) Scans are converted to pixels
   (c) A vector controller is required
   (d) a and c
   (e) a, b, and c
7. Which of the following is (are) true for a vector scan?
   (a) The scan can draw lines and characters
   (b) A vector controller is required
   (c) Flicker is present
   (d) a and c
   (e) a, b, and c

8. Which of the following is not an application of computer graphics?
   (a) Entertainment
   (b) Visualization
   (c) Education
   (d) Physical training
9. Ray tracers
   (a) Operate by tracing theoretical light rays as they intersect objects in the scene and the projection plane
   (b) Operate on an object-by-object basis, directly drawing each polygon to the screen
   (c) Are processor intensive
   (d) a and b
   (e) a and c
10. Scan-line renderers
   (a) Operate on an object-by-object basis, directly drawing each polygon to the screen
   (b) Operate by tracing theoretical light rays as they intersect objects in the scene and the projection plane
   (c) Use Gouraud shading
   (d) a and c
   (e) a and b

References

1. Ralf Steinmetz and Klara Nahrstedt, *Multimedia: Computing, Communications and Applications*, New Delhi, India: Pearson Education, 1995.
2. Ze-Nian Li and Mark S. Drew, *Fundamentals of Multimedia*, New Delhi, India: Pearson Education, 2004.
3. Prabhat K. Andleigh and Kiran Thakrar, *Multimedia Systems Design*, New Delhi, India: Pearson Education, 1996.
4. Department of Higher Education, Karnataka State Open University, Msiy121D, Multimedia_ and_Animation.pdf, http://164.100.133.129:81/econtent/Uploads/MSIT121D_Multimedia_and_Animation.pdf (accessed August 2018).
5. Kay Vaughan, *Multimedia: Making it work*, New York: McGraw-Hill, 2004.
6. SRM university, Multi_systems.pdf http://www.srmuniv.ac.in/sites/default/files/files/Multimedia%20Systems.pdf (accessed July 2015).

7. Donald Hearn and M. Pauline Baker, *Computer Graphics*, New Delhi, India: Pearson Education, 2012.
8. Alexander Hornung, Ellen Dekkers and Leif Kobbelt, Character animation from 2D pictures and 3D motion data, *ACM Transactions on Graphics*, 25, 1–9, 2007.
9. Technopedia, Character Animation, https://www.techopedia.com/definition/100/character-animation (accessed September 2018).
10. Timothy Hykes, 2d Motion Graphics Tutorials, https://www.pinterest.com/timhykes/2d-motion-graphics-tutorials/ (accessed September 2018).

7

Multimedia Data Compression

7.1 Introduction

Data compression is one of the most important requirements in the development of multimedia. The need for data compression in computers is a consequence of the limitations of available memory storage capacity and processing capability [1–6]. The need for data compression is also prompted by the following three factors:

1. Representation of multimedia data
2. Storage and processing of data
3. Transmission of multimedia information

Some examples give an idea of representation, storage, and transmission requirements for various multimedia elements. A grayscale image of dimension 320 × 240 × 8 bits requires 77 Kb (kilobytes) of storage. A color image of 1100 × 900 pixels and 24 bits color requires 3 Mb (megabytes), and color video with 640 × 480 and 24-bit color having a transmission rate of 30 fps requires 27.6 Mb. For color video of 640 × 480 pixels and 24 bits color with a transmission rate of 30 frames per second (fps), a transmission rate of 27.6 Mb per second is required. High-definition television (HDTV; 1920 × 1080 pixels, 24 bits color, 30 fps) requires 1.5 Gb/sec; for cable TV, the typical transmission rate is 18 Mb/sec. For audio CD, a rate of 1.4 Mb/sec is required. For cinema quality audio with six channels, the transmission rate is 1 Gb/hour.

To understand why compression is necessary, one must distinguish between data and information [7]. Data is *not* synonymous with information. The latter is expressed through data, so its volume content can exceed the amount of information. Data that provides no relevant information is called *redundant data* or *redundancy*. The goal of multimedia coding or compression is to reduce the amount of data by reducing the amount of redundancy. Different types of redundancies are discussed in a later section.

Compression is a procedure to effectively reduce the total number of bits needed to represent certain information. There are three steps in compression and retrieval of data:

- The encoder compresses the input data.
- The compressed data is then stored or transmitted via networks.
- The decoder then decompresses the output data to retrieve the original data.

7.2 Data and Information

Data and information [7] do not have the same connotation.

Data is how information is expressed. The amount of data can exceed the amount of information.

Data that provide no relevant information is termed as *redundant data* or *redundancy*.

The objective of image coding or compression is to reduce the amount of data by reducing the amount of redundancy.

Let n_1 = data and n_2 = data – redundancy (that is, data after compression). Then we have the following definitions:

$$\textbf{Compression ratio} = CR = n_1/n_2$$

$$\textbf{Relative redundancy} = RD = 1 - 1/CR$$

To emphasize the need for compression, four typical multimedia elements are examined to understand their memory space requirements. For a textbook containing 900 pages and an average of 40 lines per page, with each line containing 75 characters, including spaces, the file size would be 900 × 40 × 75 = 2.7 million characters. If 8 bits (= 1 byte) are required per character, then the storage space required to store the book in digital form would be 21.6 Mb, or 2.7 million bytes. Thus, with a 56-kbps modem, it would take 6.5 minutes. In computers, text can be compressed in the Windows operating system (OS) using the WinZip software tool, or gzip or compress in the Unix OS. For audio using a sampling frequency of 44.1 kHz and 16 bits/sample/channel and two stereo channels, the uncompressed bit rate would be 44100 × 16 × 2 bits per sec, which equals 1.41 Mbps. To transmit this signal through a 56-kbps modem, a compression factor of 1.41 Mbps/56 kbps = 25.2, would be desirable. For a color image of 640 × 480 pixels with a 24 (8 × 3) bit true color, the space required would be 640 × 480 × 8 × 3 bits, or approximately 7.37 Mb, and would take 2.2 minutes to be transmitted through a 56-kbps modem. For videos displaying 30 such image frames per second, the space required would be 30 times as much, which is around 221 Mb per second. Thus, for both storage and transmission purposes, compression of these various forms of multimedia are essential. To achieve compression, the redundancies present in these multimedia elements must be removed during the encoding process. This encoding process involves the use of coding through codewords. If the coding process permanently removes some information (that is, the information cannot be retrieved during decoding), the compression scheme is a lossy one; otherwise it is lossless. In the next section, the various types of redundancies present in these multimedia elements are explored.

7.2.1 Redundancies

Redundancies usually mean information that is not essential. They may be blank spaces in text, long pauses in audio signals, uniform background of a blue sky in an image, to name a few. Since most multimedia information, for instance, in audio or image and video, involves the human senses of hearing and sight, audio signals or image details that cannot be distinguished by the human senses are also regarded as redundant information. Pixel intensity values are symbols in the case of image and video. Types of redundancies [3,7] present in different multimedia are as follows:

1. *Statistical redundancies*: Statistical redundancies refer to non-uniform probabilities of occurrences of the symbols of the multimedia type. For text, these symbols refer to the characters of text. Audio samples constitute the symbols of audio. Pixel intensity values are symbols in the case of image and video. Symbols occurring more frequently are given a larger number of bits than less probable symbols.
2. *Knowledge redundancies*: When a signal is limited in scope, common knowledge can be associated with it at both the encoder and decoder. The encoder transmits only the necessary information required for reconstruction. For music signals, the names of different instruments in an orchestra and how they are played can be stored. Thus, excellent quality music can be stored at a very low bit rate. This is utilized in musical instrument digital interface (MIDI). In model-based video encoding, images of people involved in teleconferencing are sent to opposite sides, thus achieving a very high compression ratio.
3. *Temporal redundancies*: For time-varying signals (temporal multimedia elements), there is often a strong correlation between neighboring sample values. This inter-sample redundancy can be removed by techniques like predictive coding and transform coding.

4. *Spatial redundancies*: In images and video, there is a correlation between neighboring pixels. This is referred to as spatial redundancy or interpixel redundancy. It can be removed by predictive coding and transform coding.
5. *Psychovisual redundancies*: The human visual system has a limited resolution (approximately 32 gray levels) and does not uniformly respond to all information with equal sensitivity. Information of relatively less importance is called psychovisual redundant information and can thus be eliminated without introducing any significant difference in visual perception. This process is referred to as quantization. Removal of psychovisual redundancies involves elimination of data and therefore is a lossy process.
6. The *psychoacoustic model* gives rise to another redundancy in audio. Psychoacoustics, as explained in Chapter 3 deals with sound perception in humans and is based on the concept of perceptual coding. The principle underlying this coding is to eliminate information from audio signals that are inaudible to the human ear.

7.2.2 Basics of Information Theory

Consider an information source S, which is a discrete memoryless function, producing statistically independent characters. This source has an alphabet $S = \{s_1, s_2, \ldots, s_k\}$, with K symbols. A character in this sequence is any one of the symbols of the alphabet. A character sequence $x[i]$ consists of N samples with $\leq i \leq N$. Here x is a random variable whose histogram is a discrete function $h[k] = n_k$, with n_k being the number of characters represented by the symbol s_k. The function $p[k]$ gives the probability of occurrence of the symbol s_k and is defined as the probability density function (pdf) of x. The function $p[k]$ is defined mathematically as:

$$p[k] = \frac{h[k]}{N}$$

The summation of all probabilities of occurrences of all symbols is unity, that is:

$$\sum_{k=0}^{K-1} p[k] = 1$$

All the K symbols are not equally important, and some are used more frequently than others.

The average information carried by a symbol is the log of the reciprocal of its probability, that is, the term log(1/*p*[*k*]), which denotes the number of bits needed to encode s_k.

Entropy provides a measure of the disorder in a system. Negative entropy is added to reduce the disorder in a system.

According to Shannon, the entropy of a source is the average amount of information per source symbol and is mathematically expressed as:

$$H(s) = -\sum_{k=1}^{K} p[k]\log_2 p[k]$$

Logarithm is to the base 2 because the information is represented as bits per symbol. The first order entropy (FOE) is a memoryless entropy defined on a sample-by-sample basis. The FOE gives the minimum bit rate required for the lossless reproduction of a sequence of discrete data.

A consequence of Shannon's noiseless coding theorem is that a source can be coded in a lossless manner, with an average bit rate greater than or equal to the entropy.

7.3 Coding

Some of the simplest coding techniques are entropy-based coding to reduce statistical redundancies. Notable examples of entropy-based coding are run-length coding (RLC) and variable-length coding (VLC). RLC is one of the simplest compression schemes that use information sources consisting of symbols forming continuous groups. As the name suggests, VLC uses variable-length codes, with frequently occurring symbols being encoded with shorter codewords and less frequent symbols occupying longer codewords. The Shannon-Fano algorithm, Huffman algorithm, and arithmetic coding are the best-known examples in this category. These coding techniques are lossless and do not consider the specific characteristics of the media. These schemes are useful for image and video.

Unlike entropy, source-coding methods incorporate the semantics of the data and can exploit spatial, temporal, and psychoacoustic models or psychovisual redundancies. The amount of compression depends on the data contents. Source coding can be both lossy or lossless, although most methods are lossy. This category includes predictive coding techniques like differential pulse code modulation (DPCM); transform coding techniques like fast Fourier transform (FFT) and discrete Fourier transform (DFT); layered coding techniques like sub-band coding; and quantization techniques, which are carried out above the Nyquist frequency. DPCM is a predictive coding technique used for compressing audio signals by exploiting temporal redundancy. In DPCM, the audio signal can be predicted from previous samples. Delta modulation (DM) is a modification of DPCM.

Hybrid coding incorporates both entropy coding as well as source coding. Examples are JPEG, MPEG, and H261, which are used in audio, image, and video compression.

Dictionary coding techniques exploit knowledge redundancies. The LZW and LZ77 algorithms are typical examples. These coding schemes are well suited for text compression.

In transform coding methods, data is transformed from one mathematical domain to another. A typical example is the Fourier transformation, which transforms data from the time domain to the frequency domain. Examples in this category are FFT, DFT, discrete cosine transform (DCT), and wavelet transform (WT).

Sub-band coding is a layered coding technique that, instead of transforming all data into another domain, performs selective frequency transformation using a spectral selection of signals in predefined frequency bands. As discussed in Chapter 3, the choice of the number of bands is important. This type of coding is used for compressing audio.

Quantization is a lossy compression scheme. The source might contain many output values or even an infinite number of values, as in the case of analog signals. However, the human ear or eye can only distinguish between a finite number of values. Hence, the set of values needs to be reduced to a smaller set using quantization. The quantizer is an algorithm that decides on the partition, both on the encoder side and decoder side. In uniform scalar quantization, the partitions are made at equally spaced intervals, with the end points of the partition called decision boundaries. However, if the input source is not uniformly distributed, a non-uniform scalar quantization can be performed. Vector quantization (VQ) is essentially scalar quantization extended to multiple dimensions. An n-component code vector represents vectors comprising of values lying within a region in n-dimensional sample space. A collection of these code vectors constitutes a codebook. Because quantization resamples values of signals into a smaller number of bins, information is lost; thus, it is a lossy scheme.

7.3.1 Run-Length Coding (RLC)

Run-length coding (RLC) is based on entropy coding and exploits statistical redundancies. It is one of the simplest coding techniques. If the information source to be compressed consists of symbols that tend to form continuous groups, then instead of compressing each symbol individually, one such symbol and the length of the group can be coded. Every codeword is made

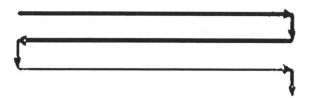

FIGURE 7.1
Direction of run-length coding.

up of a pair (g, l) where g is the gray level/symbol value, and l is the number of pixels/symbols with that gray level/symbol value (length). For example, the source described by the set of values given below:

80 80 80 56 56 56 83 80

56 56 56 56 56 56 80 80

creates the run-length code (80, 3) (56, 3) (83, 1) (80, 3) (56, 6). The code is calculated row by row in the direction indicated in Figure 7.1.

In this coding technique, knowledge of the position and image dimensions must be stored with the coded image. This is a very simple yet efficient method for coding binary images. This technique is used in fax machines.

7.3.2 Shannon-Fano Algorithm

The Shannon-Fano algorithm is another entropy coding technique that exploits statistical redundancies. It uses a top-down approach and is an application of the variable-length coding approach that assigns shorter codewords to symbols that occur more frequently. The symbols are sorted according to their frequency of occurrence. A binary tree is created by recursively dividing the symbols into two parts, with each part having approximately the same number of counts until all parts have just one symbol. An example is shown in Figure 7.2 for the word LABEL. Here there are five words, with L repeated twice. Hence, the probability $p[k]$ for L is 0.4, while the probability $p[k]$ for the other three letters A, B, and E is 0.2 each. The information content for L, using $\log_2 p[k]$, is 1.32 and for the other three letters is (using $\log_2 p[k]$) 2.32 for each letter.

The entropy H(S) is 1.92. So the minimum average number of bits per symbol should be greater than or equal to 1.92. In actual practice, two bits per sample are used. For linear coding three bits per sample would be used, resulting in 15 bits (Table 7.1).

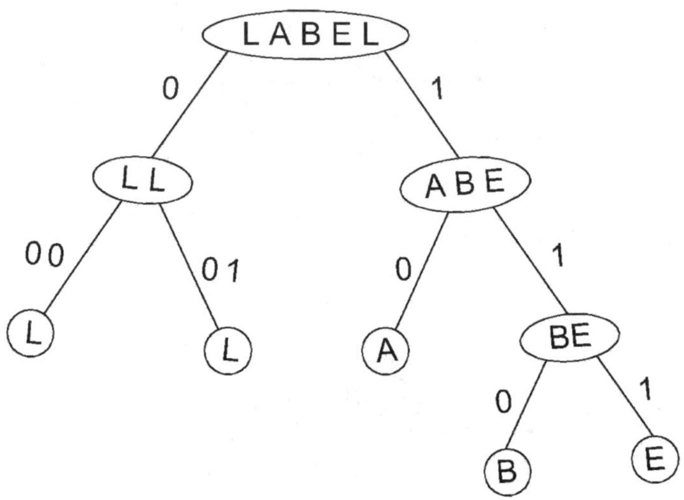

FIGURE 7.2
Shannon-Fano algorithm example.

TABLE 7.1
Symbols and Code Lengths for the Shannon-Fano Algorithm for LABEL

Symbol	Frequency	Code	Bits Used
L	2	00	2
A	1	10	2
B	1	110	3
E	1	111	3
Total number of bits 10			

7.3.3 Huffman Algorithm

The Huffman algorithm is another entropy-coding algorithm using a bottom-up approach. The following example is a data source containing the word LABEL. The symbol's frequencies are shown in Table 7.2.

The two rarest symbols E and B are connected first. This resulting node along with the node labeled A are at the next level of hierarchy. The new parent nodes have frequencies of 2 and 1, respectively, and are brought together in the next step. The resulting node and the remaining symbol L are subordinated to the root node that is created in a final step. The codes assigned are computed from the root node. So E is coded as 111, B is coded as 110, A is coded as 10, and L is coded as 00. The result for the Huffman algorithm is the same as Shannon-Fano for this simple example (Figure 7.3).

TABLE 7.2
Frequency of Symbols Used in Huffman Algorithm Example

Symbol	Frequency
L	2
A	1
B	1
E	1

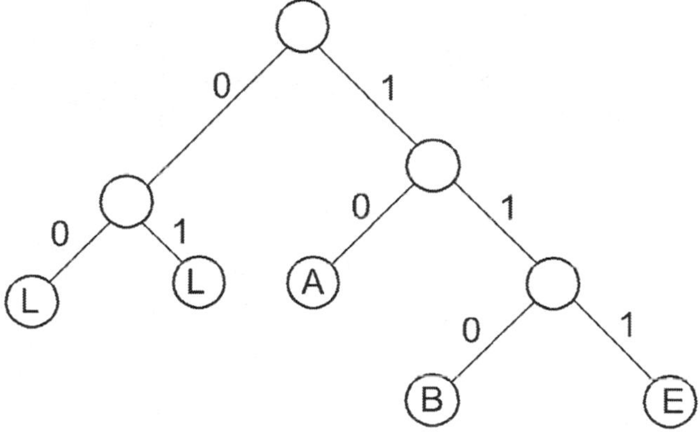

FIGURE 7.3
Code tree of Huffman algorithm for LABEL.

7.3.4 Arithmetic-Coding Algorithm

Arithmetic coding is one of the most efficient methods for coding. This technique also codes symbols according to the probability of their occurrence. The average code length conforms exactly to the possible minimum obtained from information theory and there are no deviations due to bit resolution of binary code trees. Unfortunately, the usage is restricted by patents. Using arithmetic coding without acquiring a license is prohibited.

In contrast to a binary Huffman code tree, arithmetic coding offers a clearly better compression rate, although its implementation is more cumbersome. It is the method of choice for JPEG compression and is based on entropy coding. Despite its lower efficiency, Huffman coding remains the standard due to the legal restrictions mentioned above.

The entire data set is represented by a single rational number, which is between 0 and 1, and divided into sub-intervals. Each sub-interval represents a certain symbol of the given string, with the size of this interval determined by the probability of its occurrence. For each symbol in the original data, a new interval division takes place, based on the last sub-interval.

A message is given by a half open interval [a, b), where a and b are real numbers between 0 and 1. In the next stage, b is encoded, with a occupying 50% of the interval [0.5;0.8), thus giving rise to a narrower interval [0.50;0.65); b occupies 30% of the next slot to give an interval of [0.65;0.74); and the last slot is occupied by c with 20% giving [0.74;0.80) (Figure 7.4). The process is repeated with the symbol a occupying 50% of the interval [0.5;0.8) to give [0.5;0.65), and so on. The intervals are shown in Table 7.3.

Starting with the initial subdivision, the symbol b is coded with a number, which is greater than or equal to 0.5 and less than 0.8. If the symbol b would stand alone, any number from this interval could be selected.

The encoding starts with the current interval [0.5;0.8), which will be divided again into sub-intervals, and the process is repeated until the string terminates. The number of significant digits of the codeword increases continuously. The decoding process is illustrated in Figure 7.5.

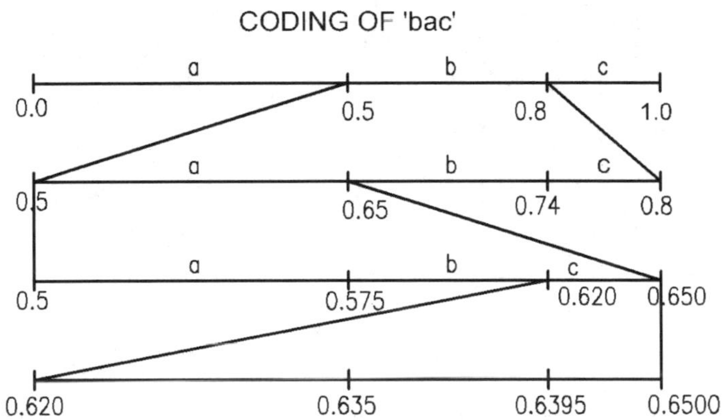

FIGURE 7.4
Arithmetic coding for bac.

TABLE 7.3
Encode Symbols 'bac'

Symbol	Probability	Interval
a	0.5	[0.0; 0.5)
b	0.3	[0.5; 0.8)
c	0.2	[0.8; 1.0)

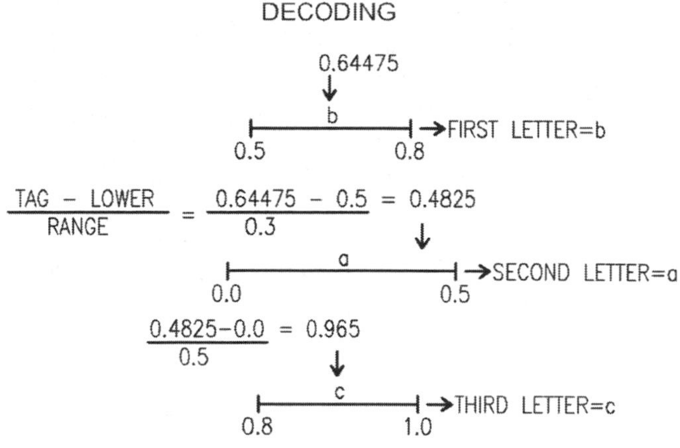

FIGURE 7.5
Arithmetic decoding of bac.

7.3.5 Higher-Order Models

To compress a source of several characters, a source alphabet that includes a set of all possible values of the characters needs to be defined. For example, consider a source denoted by $X = (x_1, x_2, x_3,\ldots)$, where x_1, x_2, and so on, are the characters of the source. A source alphabet says $A = \{a, b, c,\ldots\}$ is defined. The characters of the source, that is, $(x_i, i = 1,2,\ldots)$ are regarded as random variables of the alphabet A. The source is an infinite sequence of random variables, so X is just a random process. Entropy rate is the fundamental limit to lossless data compression and is denoted by the symbol H. The entropy rate of the source is a number that depends only on the statistical nature of the source. There are several ways of modeling the statistical properties of the source, as described below:

Zero order model: Each character or sample is statistically independent of all other characters.

Entropy rate $H = \log_2 m$ bit/character, where m is the size of the alphabet.

First-order model: The characters or samples from the source are still independent of one another, but the probability distributions of characters are based on a first-order statistical distribution (since some characters are more probable than others):

$$H = -\sum_{i=1}^{m} p_i \log_2 p_i \text{ bits/character}$$

where m is the size of alphabet and P_i is the probability of its ith letter.

Second-order model: The probability distribution of characters or samples of source names according to what the previous character is:

$$H = -\sum_{i=1}^{m} p_i \sum_{j=1}^{n} p_{j|i} \log_2 p_{j|i} \text{ bits/character}$$

where $P_{j|i}$ is the conditional probability that the present character is the *j*th letter if the previous character is the *i*th letter.

Third-order model: The third-order model is an extension of the previous model. The present character of the source depends on the previous two characters but is independent of all previous characters before those:

$$H = -\sum_{i=1}^{m} p_i \sum_{j=1}^{n} p_{i|j} \sum_{k-1}^{l} p_{k|j,i} \log_2 p_{k|j,i} \text{ bits/character}$$

General model: Treat the source as a stationary random process. This model is too complex:

$$H = \lim_{n \to \infty} \frac{1}{n} \Sigma p(B_n) \log_2 P(B_n) \text{ bits/character}$$

where n represents first n characters.

7.3.5.1 Finite Context Model (FCM)

The goal of compression is to predict accurately symbols that appear more often and assign them fewer bits. Table 7.4 gives the zero-order finite context model (FCM) model.

In order 0 model (no context)

In the order one-FCM model considers the symbols that appeared after the current order 1 context. If we had to compress an *h* preceded by a *t*, for example, there, that, the, we would use past problem, but only when t is preceded.

TABLE 7.4

Zero Order FCM Example for bacb

Symbol	Frequency	Problems
a	1	1/4
b	2	2/4
c	1	1/4

7.3.6 Dictionary-Based Compression

Dictionary-based compression is another data encoding method that exploits knowledge redundancy present in the data. It does not encode single symbols as variable-length code. It can encode several symbols as a single token or word.

7.3.6.1 Static Dictionary–Based Approach

The static dictionary–based approach can be used to fit the data problems. Considerations involved are:

1. How to pass dictionary from encoder to decoder.
2. Compression schemes are ad-hoc and implementation is independent.

7.3.6.2 Adaptive Dictionary–Based Approach

In the adaptive dictionary–based approach, compression begins either with no dictionary or with a default baseline dictionary. The basic principle is to pass an input text stream into fragments for testing against the dictionary. If fragments do not match, then they are added as a new word and encoded. The approach can decode an input stream into either dictionary indices or plain text and add new phrases to the dictionary program. It must convert dictionary indices into phrases and display them as plain text.

7.3.6.3 LZ77

LZ77 is a sliding window, dictionary-based algorithm that addresses byte sequences from former contents instead of the original data. All data are coded in the same form because there is generally only one coding scheme. An example is provided below.

Example

Let an input string be given by the following: ABBZZXREYTGJJJA SDERRZZXREFEERZZXURPP.

Step 1: Start with a 20-character dictionary/sliding window and an eight-character look-ahead window. Starting at the beginning of the string, one arrives at:

ABBZZXREYTGJJJASDERR ZZXREFEE

<---------20 CHAR---------> <-8 CHAR>

Step 2: Here, five characters are represented by offset length:

ABBZZXREYTGJJJASDERR| (4,5)

Step 3: With five new characters, RZZXU is moved into the look-ahead window:

XREYTGJJJASDERRZZXRE FEERZZXU

<----- Sliding window -------> <look-ahead>

There is no match for FEE, so one pushes the sliding window to enter three new characters in the look-ahead window:

YTGJJJASDERRZZXREFEE RZZXURPP

<----------20 CHAR-----------> < 8 characters >

SLIDING WINDOW LOOK-AHEAD

One finds that three characters are matched and the (offset, length) = (12,3). Hence, the final compressed output is given by,

[ABB......................DERR, (4,5), FEE, (12,3) …]

Decompression: A sliding window of identical size is required. A look-ahead window is not required. Decompress data into the sliding window when (offset, length) is detected. The decompressor points to the position of offset and begins to copy the specified number of symbols and to shift0 them into the same sliding window.

Restrictions of the algorithm: To keep the runtime and buffering capacity in an acceptable range, the addressing must be limited to a certain maximum value. Contents exceeding this range will not be considered for coding and will not be covered by the size of the addressing pointer.

Compression efficiency of the algorithm: The achievable compression rate depends only on repeating sequences. Other types of redundancy like an unequal probability distribution of the set of symbols cannot be reduced. For that reason, the compression of a pure LZ77 implementation is relatively low.

A significantly better compression rate can be achieved by combining LZ77 with an additional entropy coding algorithm, for example, the Huffman or Shannon-Fano coding. The widespread deflate compression method (e.g., for GZIP or ZIP) uses Huffman codes.

7.3.6.4 LZW Algorithm

The LZW compression method was derived from LZ78 by Jacob Ziv and Abraham Lempel and later invented by Terry A. Welch in 1984 who had published his considerations in the article "A Technique for High-Performance Data Compression." LZW is an important part of a variety of data formats. Graphic formats like gif, tiff (optional), and Postscript use LZW for entropy coding.

LZW is a dictionary-based algorithm that contains any byte sequence already coded. The compressed data exceptionally consist of indices to this dictionary. Before starting, the dictionary is preset with entries for the 256 single byte symbols. Any entry following represents sequences larger than one byte. The algorithm presented by Terry Welch defines mechanisms to create the dictionary and to ensure that it will be identical for both the encoding and decoding process.

LZW uses fixed-length codewords to represent variable-length strings of symbols and characters that commonly occur together, for example, words in English text. The LZW encoder and decoder build up the same dictionary dynamically while receiving the data. LZW places longer and longer repeated entries into a dictionary, and then emits the code for an element, rather than the string itself, if the element has already been placed in the dictionary.

We will compress the string XYXYYXYZXYXYYX. The initial dictionary is given in Table 7.5. The string XY is not in the initial dictionary, so it is added with code index 4. The next string YX is also added as a new entry. The rest of the strings are incorporated in the new dictionary as indicated in Table 7.6, and the pseudocode for encoding is provided in Figure 7.3. The string XYXYYXYZXBBX is thus encoded as <1><2><4><5><2><3><4><6><1>.

In the decompression process, the strings are decoded from the same dictionary using the index numbers assigned in this dictionary. The code indices given in column 2 of Table 7.6 are decoded as output given in column 3 of Table 7.7.

TABLE 7.5

LZW Dictionary

Code	String
1	X
2	Y
3	Z

TABLE 7.6

New Dictionary of LZW

Input	Next Input	Output	Code	String
			1	X
			2	Y
			3	Z
X	Y	1	4	XY
Y	X	2	5	YX
X	Y			
XY	Y	4	6	XYY
Y	X			
YX	Y	5	7	YXY
Y	Z	2	8	YZ
Z	X	3	9	ZX
X	Y			
XY	X	4	10	XYX
X	Y			
XY	Y			
XYY	X	6	11	XYYX
X	EOF	1		

TABLE 7.7
Output Dictionary for LZW

Input	Next Input	Entry/Output	Code	String
			1	X
			2	Y
			3	Z
NIL	1	X		
X	2	Y	4	XY
Y	4	XY	5	YX
XY	5	YX	6	XYY
YX	2	Y	7	YXY
Y	3	Z	8	YZ
Z	4	XY	9	ZX
XY	6	XYY	10	XYX
XYY	1	X	11	XYYX
X	EOF			

7.4 Transform Coding

Transform coding converts data into a form where compression is simpler to implement. This transformation changes the symbols, which are correlated into a representation where they are decorrelated. The new values are usually smaller on average than the original values. The net effect is to reduce the redundancy of the representation. The transform coefficients can then be quantized according to their statistical properties, producing a much-compressed representation of the original data. Because this coding technique eliminates data, it is a lossy process. Some popular transform coding techniques are DCT and discrete wavelet transform, which will be discussed in the following section.

7.4.1 Discrete Fourier Transform (DFT)

DFT essentially converts a finite set of equally spaced samples of a function into a list of coefficients of a finite set of complex sinusoids ordered by their frequencies that have the same sample values. The sampled function is converted from the original domain (e.g., the time domain or the spatial domain) into the frequency domain. The two-dimensional (2D) DFT and its inverse are defined below.

The 2D DFT:

$$f(x,y)=\sum_{u=0}^{N-1}\sum_{v=0}^{M-1}F(u,v)e^{+2\pi i\left(\frac{ux}{N}+\frac{vy}{M}\right)}$$

with $f(x, y)$ equal to the original signal in the spatial (that is, x, y) domain and F(u, v) equal to the transformed signal in the u, v domain. Here, $x = 0, 1, N{-}1$ and $y = 0, 1,..., M{-}1$ and u = 0, 1,..., $N{-}1$ and $v = 0, 1,..., M{-}1$.

The inverse transformation is defined as:

$$F(u,v)=\frac{1}{N}\frac{1}{M}\sum_{u=0}^{N-1}\sum_{v=0}^{M-1}f(x,y)e^{+2\pi i\left(\frac{ux}{N}+\frac{vy}{M}\right)}$$

The kernel of the DFT involves complex numbers, and so the computation is complex.

7.4.2 Discrete Cosine Transform (DCT)

A finite sequence of data points can be expressed in terms of a sum of cosine functions oscillating at different frequencies using DCT. DCT is essentially a Fourier-related transform using only real numbers. The DCTs are equivalent to DFTs of roughly double the length, operating on data with even symmetry. Since computations are on real numbers only, DCT is advantageous over DFT where computations are performed on complex numbers. The 2D DCT is defined as:

$$b(u,v)=\frac{2}{N}C(u)C(v)\sum_{x=0}^{N-1}\sum_{y=0}^{M-1}a(x,y)\cos\left\{\frac{\pi u(2x+1)}{2N}\right\}\cos\left\{\frac{\pi v(2y+1)}{2M}\right\}$$

The inverse 2D DCT (IDCT) is defined as:

$$a(x,y)=\frac{2}{N}\sum_{x=0}^{N-1}\sum_{y=0}^{M-1}C(u)C(v)b(u,v)\cos\left\{\frac{\pi u(2x+1)}{2N}\right\}\cos\left\{\frac{\pi v(2y+1)}{2M}\right\}$$

where:

$$C(u)=\begin{cases}\frac{1}{\sqrt{2}}, & |\,u=0\\ 1, & |\text{ otherwise}\end{cases}$$

DCT ia used in JPEG compression, which is described in the next section.

7.5 JPEG Compression

JPEG is an image compression [1–3] standard developed by the Joint Photographic Experts Group (JPEG) of the ISO/IEC. It is used for the coding and compression of color as well as grayscale images. It is generally a lossy compression standard. JPEG is an effective image compression standard because (1) image data changes slowly across an image, specially an 8 × 8 data block, and therefore there is much interpixel redundancy; (2) it has been observed that humans are not very sensitive to high-frequency data images, and thus redundancy in data can be removed by transform coding; and (3) humans are much more sensitive to brightness (luminance) than color (chrominance). Thus, a chroma subsampling of (4:2:0) can be used. JPEG compression includes the following steps (Figure 7.6):

1. RGB images are converted to YIQ or YUV and color is subsampled.
2. A DCT is performed on 8 × 8 blocks of the image.

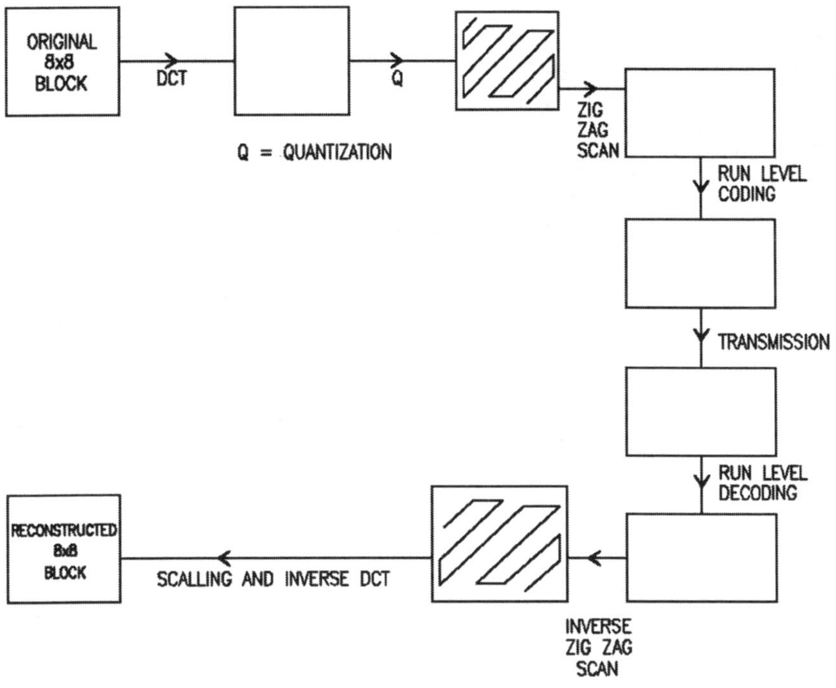

FIGURE 7.6
Schematic of JPEG compression and decompression.

3. Quantization is performed on the pixel values.
4. Subsequently, zigzag ordering and run-length encoding is performed.
5. Finally, entropy encoding (Huffman coding) is performed.

Quantization is performed to reduce the number of bits needed for encoding. Each entry in the frequency space block is divided by an integer and then rounded. This step is performed using a quantization matrix, Q, given below:

$$\hat{F}(u,v) = round\left(\frac{F(u,v)}{Q(u,v)}\right)$$

Larger entries are used in Q for higher spatial frequencies.

Although JPEG is a lossy compression technique, the latest standard of JPEG, namely, JPEG 2000, is a lossless variant. JPEG 2000 uses wavelet technology.

7.6 Wavelets

A wavelet is a small wave or a waveform of limited duration with an average value of zero. First introduced by Haar, wavelet transforms have several advantages over the Fourier transform.

In the Fourier transform (FT), the signal is represented in terms of sinusoids of varying frequency over the entire signal range. The Fourier transformed signal is localized only in the frequency domain and not in the time domain.

In WT, basis functions vary in frequency (called scale) as well as spatial extent. High-frequency basis covers a smaller area, and low-frequency basis covers a larger area. The definition of wavelet functions provides flexibility. Wavelets can be derived from a mother wavelet. The wavelet function has the functional form:

$$\Psi_{a,bx,by}(x,y) = \frac{1}{a}\Psi\left(\frac{x-bx}{a} \quad \frac{y-by}{a}\right)$$

where:

a is the scale coefficient

bx and *by* are shift coefficients

7.7 Video Compression

A video is a sequence of images, known as frames, that are stacked in temporal dimension. The contents of consecutive frames do not change much, so videos have both spatial and temporal redundancies [1–3]. Not every frame needs to be coded independently; only the difference between the two frames is encoded. The main cause for the difference between consecutive frames is due to camera motion or object motion, or both. Thus, a motion compensation procedure must be performed. Motion generators can be compensated by detecting the displacement of corresponding pixels or regions and measuring differences. This procedure, termed motion compensation (MC), takes place in three steps. In the first step, motion estimation is carried out to search for a motion vector (MV). This is followed by the motion-compensation based prediction. In the third step, the prediction error is computed.

Each image is subdivided into macro-blocks of size N × N, where N has a typical value of 16 for luminance images. For chrominance images, chroma subsampling is performed. This chroma subsampling consists of sampling the pixels at regular intervals for chrominance values. The human eye is less sensitive to color than form, so the chrominance signal is decimated. This process consists of giving numbers stating how many pixel values of the chrominance components per original four pixels need to be sent. Usually, when four luminance values sent, only the chrominance components of the even pixels are sent. Motion compensation is performed at the macro-block level. The image frame to be compared is called the target frame, while the previous frame or succeeding frame with whom the comparison is made is called the reference frame. The displacement between the target macro-frame and the reference macro-frame is the motion vector. The difference between the target macro-block and the reference macro-frame is the prediction error.

For high-compression ratios, redundancies of neighboring frames (that is, interframes) are exploited. This is done for P-frames (predictive-coded frames). Fast random access demands temporal intraframe (or I-frame) coding. B-frame (bidirectional) predictive coding requires information from both previous and following I frames and/or P-frames. D-frames are DC-coded frames that are intraframe coded. MPEG compression in videos uses these four types of coding for compression and image processing.

Review

At the end of this chapter you will have learned about the following topics:

The distinction between data and information

Different types of redundancies

Lossy and lossless coding techniques

Entropy-based coding techniques: Shannon-Fano, Huffman, higher-order models, arithmetic coding, and run-length coding

Dictionary based coding: LZ77 and LZW

Transform-based coding: DFT, DCT, and wavelet transform

JPEG compression

Review Questions

1. What is the difference between data and information?
2. Discuss the different types of redundancies in multimedia data.
3. What is lossless and lossy compression?
4. Describe briefly the following different types of entropy coding and give examples wherever possible: Shannon-Fano, Huffman, arithmetic coding, higher-order models, FCM, run-length coding.
5. Describe the two dictionary-based coding techniques, LZ77 and LZW
6. What is transform coding? Discuss DFT, DCT, and wavelet transform.
7. How is JPEG compression achieved?

Multiple-Choice Questions

1. In compression, input data is coded via the:
   (a) Decoder
   (b) Encoder
   (c) Networks
   (d) None of the above
2. In an 8×8 image requiring three bits per pixel and compressed image of the same dimension requiring 2.32 bits per pixel, the compression ratio is:
   (a) 1.29
   (b) 0.77
   (c) 1
   (d) None of the above

3. Statistical redundancies are associated with:
   (a) Non-uniform occurrence of symbols
   (b) Common knowledge associated with encoder and decoder
   (c) Time varying signals
   (d) All of the above
   (e) None of the above
4. Lossy compression is involved with removing:
   (a) Coding redundancies
   (b) Interpixel redundancies
   (c) Psychovisual redundancies
   (d) All of the above
   (e) None of the above

Problems

1. For an alphabet A = {a, e, i, o, u, y} with probabilities 0.3,0.2,0.2, 0.1,0.1,0.1, respectively, draw the Shannon-Fano and Huffman trees.
2. For the probability model in the table below, find the arithmetic code for the sequence abcba.

   Symbol Probability
   (a) 0.2
   (b) 0.3
   (c) 0.5

   Answer: 0.0246
3. For the 4 × 4.8 bit image given by:
   (a) 24 24 116 116
   (b) 24 24 116 116
   (c) 24 24 116 116
   (d) 24 24 116 116

   develop a dictionary using the LZW algorithm.
4. Consider a 16-character sliding window and a five-character look-ahead window. Encode the sequence given in the above problem using the LZ 77 technique.

   (String ABBZZXREYTGJJJASDERRZZXREFEERZZXURPP)

Solutions to Problems

Answer to Problem 1:

SHANNON-FANO

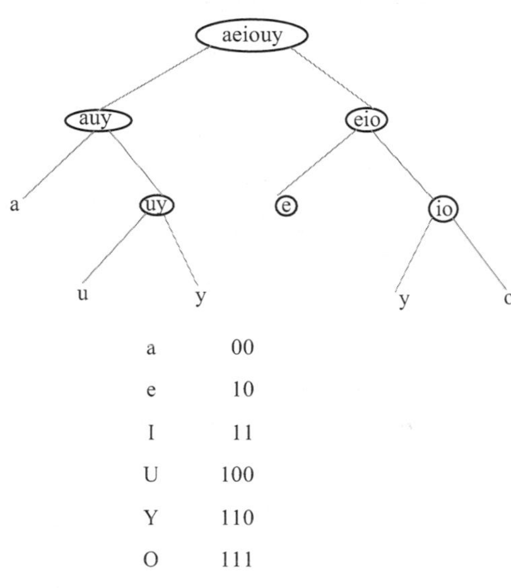

a	00
e	10
I	11
U	100
Y	110
O	111

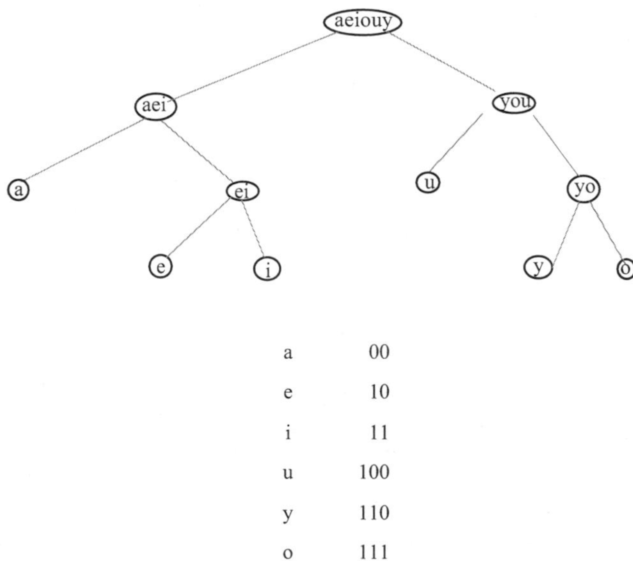

a	00
e	10
i	11
u	100
y	110
o	111

Answer to Problem 2: Code abcba

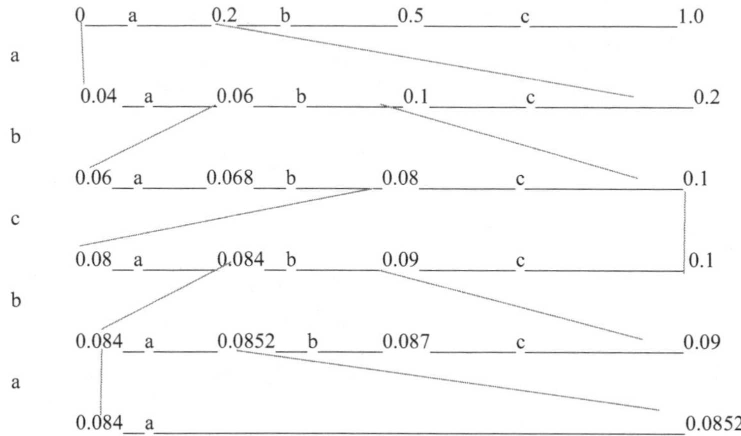

$$\text{Tag value} = \frac{0.084 + 0.0852}{2} = 0.0846 = \text{code}$$

Answer to Problem 3:

Current Sequence	Pixel Being Processed	Encoded Output	Dictionary Location (Codeword)	Dictionary Entry
	24			
24	24	24	256	24-24
24	116	24	257	24-116
116	116	116	258	116-116
116	24	116	259	116-24
24	24			
24-24	116	256	260	24-24-116
116	116			
116-116	24	258	261	116-116-24
24	24			
24-24	116			
24-24-116	116	260	262	24-24-116-116
116	24			
116-24	24	259	263	116-24=24
24	116			
24-116	116	257	264	24-116-116
116		116		

Answer to Problem 4:

String: ABBZZXREYTGJJJASDERRZZXREFEERZZXURPP
Dictionary/Sliding Window (16 characters)
ABBZZXREYTGJJJAS
5-character sliding window:
DERRZ
Final compressed output:
[ABBZZXREYTGJJJAS, DERR, (4,5), REFEE, (12,4) ...]

References

1. Ralf Steinmetz and Klara Nahrstedt, *Multimedia: Computing, Communications and Applications*, New Delhi, India: Pearson Education, 1995.
2. Ze-Nian Li and Mark S. Drew, *Fundamentals of Multimedia*, New Delhi, India: Pearson Education, 2004.
3. Mrinal K. Mandal, *Multimedia Signals and Systems*, Boston, MA: Kluwer Academic Publishers (now part of Springer Science + Business Media), 2003.
4. Prabhat K. Andleigh and Kiran Thakrar, *Multimedia Systems Design*, New Delhi, India, Pearson Education, 1996.
5. Fred Halsall, *Multimedia Communications: Applications, Networks, Protocols and Standards*, New Delhi, India: Pearson Education, 2001.
6. Kay Vaughan, *Multimedia: Making it Work*, New York: McGraw-Hill, 2004.
7. Robert E. Woods and Rafael C. Gonzalez, *Digital Image Processing*, New York: Prentice Hall Technical Education, 1992.

8

Multimedia Content Creation and Presentation

8.1 Introduction

One of the most important uses of multimedia is to design and develop presentations for applications in business, communication, education, entertainment, and so on, by appropriate integration of multimedia elements, often referred to as multimedia objects [1–6]. In this chapter, the different phases of the development of a multimedia project will be outlined.

In the next section, the analysis, design, development, implementation, evaluation (ADDIE) model for project development will be presented. This will be followed by sections on multimedia authoring and authoring metaphors. Multimedia documents can be represented in a variety of ways including traditional documents, hypertext and hypermedia, so open document architecture will be discussed subsequently. Finally, a brief overview of multimedia standards will be given.

8.2 ADDIE Model

The ADDIE model describes multimedia project development in five phases: analysis, design, development, implementation, and evaluation.

The analysis phase articulates the goals of the project and the performance objectives.

The design phase then lays out a road map for accomplishing the goals and objectives.

The development phase then creates the elements laid out in the design phase.

The implementation phase is used for deploying and testing.

Finally, the evaluation phase measures whether the training works and goals have been achieved.

The **analysis** phase consists of studying the needs of the clients and end users, the required content, which technology is to be involved, and the constraints to be imposed.

8.2.1 Design Phase

The design phase includes several stages: storyboarding, flowcharting, prototyping, and user testing.

- The storyboard depicts the initial content of a multimedia concept in a series of sketches. These are analogous to key frames in video.
- The flowchart stage then organizes the storyboard by inserting navigation information, which is the multimedia's concept of structure and user interaction.
- Then a detailed functional specification, consisting of a walk-through of each scenario of the presentation, frame by frame, including all screen action and user interaction, is performed.
- The final part of the design phase is prototyping and testing.

8.3 Multimedia Authoring

After laying the road map for goals and objectives, the multimedia **development** phase, a process referred to as authoring, begins. Multimedia authoring involves the creation of multimedia productions, sometimes called movies or presentations.

8.3.1 Multimedia Authoring Metaphors

The authoring metaphor or authoring paradigm is the methodology by which the authoring or development system accomplishes its task. Some of the important metaphors are listed below:

1. Scripting Language Metaphor uses a special language to enable interactivity (buttons, mouse, and so on) and to allow conditionals, jumps, loops, functions/macros, and so on. The example below is a Lingo script for the Director software:

   ```
   on exitFrame

         go the frame

   end
   ```

   This frame script tells Director to keep playing the same frame.
2. Slide Show Metaphor is a linear presentation by default. However, there are tools to perform jumps in slide shows. An example is PowerPoint.
3. Hierarchical Metaphor deploys user-controllable elements. These are organized into a tree structure. This metaphor is often used in menu-driven applications.
4. Iconic/Flow-Control Metaphor: Here, graphical icons are available in a toolbox, and authoring proceeds by creating a flowchart with icons attached.
   - Example is Authorware, which has the following salient features:
     - It is one of the most widely used visual authoring tools for creating rich-media e-learning applications for delivery on corporate networks, CDs, DVDs, and the Web.
     - It has to the ability drag and drop icons to create a logical outline.
     - It is a flowline metaphor.
5. Frames Metaphor is like Iconic/Flow-Control Metaphor. The difference is that links between icons are more conceptual rather than representing the actual flow of the program.
6. Card/Scripting Metaphor uses a simple index-card structure. This metaphor provides an easy route to producing Cast/Score/Scripting Metaphor applications. Here, time is shown horizontally, like a spreadsheet. Rows, or **tracks**, represent instantiations of characters in a multimedia production. The multimedia elements are drawn from a **cast** of characters, and **scripts** are basically event procedures or procedures that are triggered by timer events. Director, by Macromedia, is the most prominent example of this metaphor, which uses an object-oriented, event-driven language: the **Lingo** scripting language.

8.4 Elements of Multimedia Presentations

Some of the important effects to be considered for the presentation of multimedia content are outlined below:

- **Graphics styles**: Human visual dynamics have a huge impact how presentations must be constructed. Hence, combinations of color schemes, which enhance this impact, must be chosen while keeping this in mind.
- **Color principles and guidelines**: Some color schemes and art styles are best suited to a certain theme or style. One must not use too many colors because they can be distracting.
- **Fonts**: Large fonts of 18–36 points and no more than six to eight lines per screen can be used for effective visual communication in a presentation. Also, sans-serif fonts work better than serif fonts.
- Multimedia presentations often use **sprite** animations. This technique uses a still image that describes a static background over a sequence of video frames. Here, video transitions can be used to signal scene changes. There are many different types of transitions:
  1. The easiest and most frequently used transition is **Cut**, which results in an abrupt change of image contents resulting from abutting two video frames consecutively.
  2. **Wipe** is a replacement of the pixels in a region of the viewport with those from another video. Wipes can be left to right, right to left, vertical, horizontal, swept out like the hands of a clock, and so on.
  3. In **Dissolve**, every pixel is replaced with a mixture over time of the two videos. It comes in two types: **cross dissolve** and **dither dissolve**.

8.5 Technical Design Issues

The technical design issues of developing a multimedia presentation include memory and disk space requirements and delivery methods.

8.5.1 Memory and Disk Space Requirements

For performance and storage for multimedia programs, a minimum of 128 MB of RAM and 20 GB of hard-disk space should be available.

8.5.2 Delivery Methods

Rewriteable DVD drives are the need of the hour because CD-ROMs do not have enough storage, and access time for CD-ROM drives is longer than for hard-disk drives. Electronic delivery is network bandwidth dependent, so its usage requires a large enough bandwidth. A streaming option can also be used for certain types of multimedia presentations.

8.6 Multimedia Authoring Tools

Some popular authoring tools include the following:

- Adobe Director 12 and MX (formerly Macromedia Director)
- Adobe Flash and MX
- Macromedia Dreamweaver 8 MX
  - Director is a complete environment for creating interactive movies.
  - Uses the movie metaphor, including Stage and Cast.

Each instance is called a sprite. Sprites can have behaviors attached.

- Score
- Flash is a simple authoring tool that facilitates the creation of interactive movies. With Flash, the movie can have one or more scenes. The Components of a movie are called *symbols.* These symbols are in turn placed on the stage. This stage consists of one or multiple layers. For each layer, the timeline window has one horizontal bar. The entire movie is composed of several key frames. Scripts are attached to symbols as well as keyframes.

  Dreamweaver is used to build multimedia-enabled Web sites as well as Internet applications in HTML, XML, and other formats. The characteristics include the support of WYSIWYG web page development as well as JavaScript, ASP, PHP, XML. Several prepackaged behaviors are available and are extensible.

8.7 Virtual Reality Modeling Language (VRML)

VRML was conceived at the first international conference of the World Wide Web as a platform-independent language that would be viewed on the Internet. The objective of VRML is to put colored objects into a three-dimensional (3D) environment. It is an interpreted language. It has become very popular because it was the first method available for displaying a 3D world on the World Wide Web.

VRML SHAPES are basic geometric shapes that can be combined to create more complex objects. These shapes include cubes, cones, cylinders, and polygonal shapes.

VRML NODES include a **Shape node**, which is a generic node for all objects in VRML. The **Material node** specifies the surface properties of an object and can control the color of the object by specifying the red (R), green (G), and blue (B) values of the object.

Three kinds of texture nodes that can be used to map textures onto any object. **ImageTexture**, the most common texture node, can take an external JPEG or PNG image file and map it onto the shape. The second, **MovieTexture**, allows the mapping of an MPEG movie onto an object. **PixelTexture** creates an image to use with ImageTexture within VRML.

8.8 Document Architecture

A *document* consists of a set of structural information that can be in different forms of media. During a presentation, it can be generated or recorded. Essentially, it is aimed at the perception of a human accessible for computer processing.

8.8.1 Properties of Documents

Structure, presentation style, semantics, and external action can be expressed using Syntax, which can either implicit in the documents or expressed as a language. A structural element like a section can have a Formatting Style associated with it that tells how the elements relate to each other within the document.

The document is displayed or printed using a **Presentation Style**. It can be embedded in LaTeX, documents using macros. In CSS for HTML documents, this style can be defined separately, for instance, by the author, in applications or languages, or by the reader in a Web browser.

Semantics is the meaning within a language.

Metadata is the information about the organization of the data, or data about the data. Examples included the author, publication date, subject codes, and so on.

A *multimedia document* is comprised of information coded in at least one continuous (time-dependent) medium and one discrete (time-independent) medium related to the environment of tools, data abstractions, basic concepts, and document architecture (da). Synchronization among the different multimedia elements is another feature that distinguishes a multimedia document from an ordinary document.

Currently continuous and discrete data are processed differently. For example, text is entered with an editor program as programming language. The motion picture is entered with an editor program only through library calls.

The goals of abstracting multimedia data are uniform description and processing of all media. System concepts for document processing use multimedia abstractions and serve as concepts for information architecture (ia) in a document. The terms ia and da are used interchangeably.

Exchanging documents entails exchanging document content as well as document structure. This requires both documents to have the same structure. Current standardized architectures are *Standardized General Markup Language (SGML)* and *Open Document Architecture (ODA).*

Document architecture describes connections among individual elements represented as models. There are three models:

1. The *manipulation model* for the creation, change, and deletion of multimedia information.
2. The *representation model* performs two tasks:
    a. Defines protocols for exchanging this information among different computers.
    b. Provides formats for storing the data. It includes relations between individual information elements to be considered during presentation.
3. The *presentation model* of the document, must be final and executable.

Because the content of the documents are multimedia (that is, they contain audio, video, images, and so on), it is necessary to use *synchronization* between the different media elements, especially between the temporal and non-temporal elements of the multimedia document. *Links* between different elements enable non-linear access between different data elements.

8.9 Hypermedia and Hypertext

Knowledge stored in the human brain via several media can be reproduced through communication. Knowledge transmission starts with the author and ends with the reader. Information loss is minimal.

Ordinary documents with linear form do not support reconstruction of knowledge or simplify reproduction. Knowledge must be artificially serialized before exchange; that is, it must be transformed into a linear document and structural information must be integrated into actual content.

Hypertext is an information object that includes links to several media. That is, if only links to text data are present in the information, it is referred to as hypertext. *Hypermedia* includes non-linear information links of hypertext systems and continuous and discrete media of multimedia systems. The words *hypertext* and *hypermedia* are used interchangeably in literature.

Hypertext and hypermedia have a non-linear information link; that is, there exists not only a reading sequence but also the reader decides on the reading path, so the reader can cross reference to systems.

Hypertext structure is a graph consisting of nodes and edges. Nodes are information units. Edges provide links to other units. Forward movement in linear sorted documents is called a navigation through the graph. At the user interface, the origin of pointers must be marked. This is called an *anchor.*

8.9.1 Properties of an Anchor

- Media-independent representation can happen through the selection of general graphical elements such as buttons.
- In text, individual words, paragraphs, or text sections of different lengths can be used for representations.
- Graphical objects and areas are defined as selection objects in images.
- In motion video, media-independent representations of an anchor are preferred.
- In audio, a media-independent solution is used. Short descriptive text or an image icon is preferred.

8.9.2 Role of Pointers in Hypertext

Simple pointers link two nodes of a graph. Typed pointers are also labeled:

Implicit pointers: Relations between pointers established automatically by hypertext system

Explicit pointers: Links can be expressed through pointers. These pointers can be labelled. Some examples of labels are: *to be; to present; to include; to be similar*; etc.

8.9.3 Mark-Up

In a document, anything other than content is mark-up. *Procedural* mark-up is used by typesetters to lay out instructions of how a document should look.

Anything that describes the structure of the document rather than the appearance in called *descriptive mark-up, or generic mark up*, and content is separated from style.

SGML specifies a standard method for describing the structure of the document. **Structural elements** are, for example, the title, a chapter, or a paragraph. It is an extensible Meta Language. It can support an infinite variety of document structures, for example, information bulletins, technical manuals, parts catalogs, design specifications, reports, letters, and memos.

In SGML, tags are divided into different categories:

- Descriptive mark-up (tags) describes actual structure. It is always in the following form:

  <start-tag> respectively also </end-tag>
- Entity reference provides connection to another element, as follows:

  &square x (for x^2)
- Mark-up declarations define the elements to which an entity reference refers, for example:

  <!ELEMENT paper (preamble, body, postamble)>

Instructions for other programs in text are entered through processing instructions. Thus, SGML defines a syntax for tags through a grammar that needs to be followed but does not define the semantics of these tags.

The **Document Type Definition (DTD)** describes the structure of the document (like a database schema in a database) and provides a framework of elements (chapters, headers). DTD also specifies rules for the relationship between elements; for example, a chapter header must come after the start of a chapter. A document instance is a document whose contents are tagged in conformance with DTD. Thus, DTD can be applied throughout the whole organization of the document.

Elements can also be nested in the SGML document. A document follows the rules of a DTD with the help of a parser program, which checks if the document is structurally correct. Documents can be ported to different formats for different output media (e.g., printer, screen). Style is handled separately using style sheets (e.g., cascade stylesheets).

The advantages and disadvantages of SGML are as follows:

Advantages

High-level design is clean, so this is a very pure structured document approach.

It can be easily extended to non-textual applications.

It is human readable and writable.

Disadvantages

The language syntax is cumbersome to write, imprecisely specified, and awkward to parse.

DTD is required if tag minimization is used.

For many years, SGML did not have a style sheet standard.

Further, many ad hoc solutions were produced.

Hyper Text Mark-up Language (HTML), an application of SGML, is a tagging language that can be used on the World Wide Web for text formatting and linking document using the syntax of SGML described by a DTD. HTML is not an extensible language. Authors cannot add their own tags. HTML uses CSS language (color, font, layout for Web pages), style sheets, and Frameset to partition the browser window. Some examples of HTML are as follows:

<A HREF = "http://www.amazon.com>/click here to go to amazon.com</ A> This is an example of a reference to a link.

1. <HTML>.... </HTML> Start and end of HTML page.
2. <TITLE>...</TITLE> The page title appears at left-hand top.
3. IMG SR<C ="…"> Load image at this location on the page.

8.9.4 Style Sheets

Style sheets are formal specifications of presentations and thus specify fonts, colors, layout, and so on. Mappings from a logical representation of a document to an output model can be made. Stylesheets are written in a language that resembles a programming language; they are usually declarative and have limited programming features. Examples are Cascade Style Sheets (CSS) for HTML, eXtensible Stylesheet Language (XSL) for XML, and so on.

CSS has been designed for HTML but can also be used for XML. The syntactic style and computation model have a property-value expression. Layout is flow type. Content is laid out on an infinite scroll, that is, a window with scroll bars. Every object has a display style. There are two types of style:

1. Inline: Composes nested objects into a single paragraph by breaking them into lines.
2. Block: Treats object as a separate paragraph.

Objects are laid out using margin and centering properties for horizontal positioning, and space-before and space-after properties for vertical positioning.

A feature of this presentation is cascading. This feature supports use of multiple style sheets, that is:

- Source: site → user → author
- Priority: low → high
- Last rule dominates.

So an author can always control by using high-priority.

A style sheet is a sequence of rule blocks, like the following:

```
<contextual selector> {<list of rules>}
```

A rule binds a value to a property:

```
<property>: <value>;
```

Values are strings with property-specific semantics.

Some inconsistencies can arise in this scheme, such as:

- No mathematical computation is possible, as no mathematical expressions are involved.
- It can generate content before and after elements.

The limitations of CSS are as follows:

- CSS can't reorder material; for example, in business letters, the sender's address can't appear after the signature.
- CSS has inconsistent value semantics; for example, % has different meanings for different properties.
- Lack of mathematical expressions.

8.9.5 Extensible Markup Language (XML)

XML is a slimmed-down version of SGML. An XML DTD is an SGML DTD. However, the reverse is not true. XML is designed for World Wide Web (WWW) applications and is now a WWW standard. XML syntax is widely used by other WWW standards, and it is popular as a simple database representation. XML is different from SGML for the following reasons:

- Documents can be verified without DTD.
- It eliminates certain rarely used features of SGML.

8.9.6 Open Document Architecture (ODA)

The salient feature of ODA is that it can distinguish among content, logical structure, and layout structure.

Content architecture describes for each medium the specification of elements, possible access functions, and data coding. For text, this is the character content architecture; for raster graphics, this is the geometric graphics content architecture.

Structure and presentation models describe the cooperation of information unit according to information architecture.

Layout structure specifies the representation of the document. The presentation model is a tree. Using frames, the position and size of individual layout elements are established.

Logical structure includes partitioning of the content. For example, in writing papers, the partition would be preamble-body-preamble.

8.10 Multimedia and Hypermedia Experts Group (MHEG)

With the availability of hypertext and multimedia technology, there have been major changes in document display from previous representations of text documents because output of interactive hypermedia documents should be computer supported. The presentation of a final document should be executable. The final representation in a distributed heterogeneous system environment is important. This is done by MHEG. It provides specification for documents, which include time and user interactions. Pictorial-related formats exist. Individual elements in MHEG class hierarchy exit in the form of a tree.

Review

At the end of this chapter you will have learned about the following topics:

ADDIE model for multimedia presentation

Multimedia authoring, metaphors, and authoring tools

Virtual Reality Modeling Language (VRML)

Multimedia documents

Properties of documents

Document architecture, SGML, CSS, HTML, XML, style sheets, MHEG

Review Questions

1. Describe the ADDIE model.
2. What is authoring? What is an authoring metaphor? Describe the different authoring metaphors. List some authoring tools and their salient features.
3. Discuss some effects used in multimedia presentations.
4. What is VRML?
5. Describe some important properties of documents. What do anchors and pointers do in documents?
6. What is hypermedia and hypertext?
7. Discuss the concept of markup. Explain SGML and DTD.
8. What is HTML? What is XML?
9. What are style sheets? What are their uses and properties?
10. What are the characteristics of ODA and MHEG?

Multiple-Choice Questions

1. ADDIE model stands for:
   (a) Analysis, design, development, identification, and execution
   (b) Analysis, development, data, implementation, and evaluation
   (c) Analysis, design, development, implementation, and evaluation
   (d) Analysis, design, development, implementation, and execution
2. Which of the following metaphors uses user controllable elements for organizing a tree structure?
   (a) Iconic metaphor
   (b) Hierarchical metaphor
   (c) Slide show metaphor
   (d) Frames metaphor
3. Which of the following are effects considered for multimedia presentations?
   (a) Graphics styles
   (b) Color principles and guidelines
   (c) Fonts
   (d) All of the above
   (e) None of the above

4. Which of the following is NOT a multimedia authoring tool?
   (a) Adobe Flash
   (b) Adobe Director
   (c) Macromedia Dreamweaver
   (d) Mathworks Matlab
5. The texture nodes used to map textures into an object in VRML are:
   (a) Image
   (b) Movie
   (c) Pixel
   (d) All of the above
   (e) None of the above
6. Which of the following is a property of a document?
   (a) Syntax
   (b) Semantics
   (c) Color
   (d) a, b, and c
   (e) a and b
7. Indicate whether the following statements are True (T) or False (F).
   (a) Hypertext and hypermedia have linear information links
   (b) Hypertext and hypermedia have a graph structure consisting of nodes and edges
   (c) Hypertext and hypermedia have images, graphics, audio, and video in addition to text
8. Fill in the blanks:
   (a) At the user interface, the origin of pointers is marked as ________.
   (b) Pointers link ________ of a(n) ________.
9. Which of the following is NOT a feature of SGML?
   (a) It is a markup language
   (b) It is a metalanguage
   (c) It uses tags
   (d) It distinguishes between logical structure and layout structure

References

1. Ralf Steinmetz and Klara Nahrstedt, *Multimedia: Computing, Communications and Applications,* New Delhi, India: Pearson Education, 1995.
2. Ze-Nian Li and Mark S. Drew, *Fundamentals of Multimedia,* New Delhi, India: Pearson Education, 2004.
3. Mrinal K. Mandal, *Multimedia Signals and Systems,* Boston, MA: Kluwer Academic Publishers (now part of Springer Science + Business Media), 2003.
4. Prabhat K. Andleigh and Kiran Thakrar, *Multimedia Systems Design,* New Delhi, India: Pearson Education, 1996.
5. Fred Halsall, *Multimedia Communications: Applications, Networks, Protocols and Standards,* New Delhi, India: Pearson Education, 2001.
6. Kay Vaughan, *Multimedia: Making It Work,* New York: McGraw-Hill, 2004.
7. Richard Cullata, 2018, http://www.instructionaldesign.org/models/addie/ (accessed September 2018).

9

Multimedia Storage

9.1 Introduction

Multimedia storage is an important concern in developing multimedia products because a huge amount of storage is required due to the presence of streaming media like audio and video, in addition to static media [1–6]. Even static media like images consume a substantial amount of memory space. There are two aspects of storage, namely, devices for storage as well as storage of data in databases. The first part of this chapter discusses storage devices. The latter part of this chapter describes content retrieval from databases, with special reference to images.

9.1.1 Storage Media

Some of the popular devices for multimedia storage are:

1. Magnetic media
2. Optical media
3. Flash and solid-state chip devices
4. Cloud storage
5. File systems (traditional, multimedia)

The output devices for the stored data are:

1. CD-ROM
2. DVD
3. Scanner (for capture of data)
4. Charge-coupled devices (CCDs), which are also used for data acquisition

9.1.2 Magnetic Media

Storage in magnetic media rely on magnetic technology. Discs, floppies, and tapes are coated with iron oxide. Magnetic media are stored in discs, which are again subdivided as follows:

Track: Each disc platter consists of several concentric tracks.

Region: Each disc platter is divided into n regions for some fixed n. Each region represents a wedge of the platter with angle 360/n.

Sector: A sector is part of the track that intersects a wedge; n sectors/wedge. For n number of tracks, there are n sectors or wedges.

Cylinder: The set of all tracks from all platters is called a cylinder.

For each disc platter, there is a disc arm that contains a read-write head. A read-write head is associated. A disc address is accessed by a disc controller in two steps:

1. Seek operation with which is associated a seek time.
2. A rotational operation which functions as follows: When the head is positioned over the right track, the disc spindle rotates so that the sector with the desired physical address is located directly under the read-write (r/w) head. The time taken is referred to as the rotational latency.

The transfer rate is defined as the rate at which data is read/written, and a transfer time is associated with it. The time required to read a sector is the sum of four terms, i.e., Total time to read a sector is = average seek time + average rotation time + transfer time + controller time. For 500 Gb (gigabytes) of data, the seek time is 6 ms (milliseconds). for a data transfer rate of 50 MB/s.

9.1.2.1 Advantages and Disadvantages of Magnetic Media

Magnetic media are characterized by high speeds and relatively higher costs. They are used where higher speeds are required, for example, for day-to-day operations, online cache, and online data servers. Some magnetic storage media include integrated device electronics (IDE) and/or the small computer system interface (SCSI) of earlier versions of computers. Redundant array of inexpensive discs (RAID) is another magnetic media worth mentioning.

9.1.2.2 RAID

In RAID, redundancy is added to the content of a failed disc so that it can be reconstructed. Some techniques for adding redundancy are:

1. Mirroring RAID by updating two discs on each write. This is an expensive solution, but fast disc recovery can be achieved.

2. Bit-interleaved parity helps in maintaining parity on a special check disc. When a disc fails, the disc content is restored from the check disc for a protection group.
3. Distributed block-interleaved parity can obtain higher parallelism by distributing parity information across a protection group.

9.1.3 Optical Discs

Current optical storage devices are compact discs, which are evolutions of gramophone records with the difference that they use optical recording techniques to store multimedia data. A compact disc (CD) and CD-ROM (read-only memory) is a disc that stores digital data and is made of polycarbonate substrates with circular pits and land between the pits. The disc is covered with aluminum or gold to increase reflectivity and subsequently coated with a layer of lacquer to prevent oxidation. Types of CDs are CD-R (CD-read); CD-RW (read-write); and enhanced CD, which has audio capabilities.

The head of the lens that reads CDs is called a pickup. It moves from the inside to the outside of the surface of the CD and accesses the different parts of the CD as it spins. Infrared light from a laser diode is directed at a reflecting mirror that is part of the head assembly. This head assembly in turn moves along the head of the disc and reflects the laser light through a focusing lens onto a specific point of the disc. Reflected light from the land is clear. Light reflected from the pit is diffuse.

9.1.3.1 Advantages and Disadvantages of Optical Discs

The advantages of optical discs over magnetic media are as follows:

1. They have lower cost and are removable media.
2. They are easy to use and are also durable.
3. They have random access capability.
4. There is no electromagnetic effect on the stored data.

The disadvantages compared to magnetic media are:

1. The lower speed of access compared to magnetic media.
2. Discs are easily damaged by the presence of dirt.
3. Both CD-R and CD-RW are not backward compatible.
4. Digital video disc or digital versatile disc (DVD), both R and RW, are like CDs, with some notable differences:

They are encoded in a different format.

They possess a much higher density.

They must contain a file system called the universal disc format (UDF).

They have much higher storage capabilities than CDs.

A CD-ROM driver has one platter that has a single spiral track traversed by the read head. The spiral track is divided into sectors of equal size. In a disc drive system, the disc head moves at a constant angular velocity. However, in a CD-ROM system, the disc head moves at a constant linear velocity across these tracks.

Magneto-optical discs are based on both magnetic and optical technologies and utilize ferromagnetic materials with optical recording technology described above.

9.1.4 Traditional File Systems

A *file system* is an abstract data type (ADT) for storing. accessing, retrieving, navigating, and manipulating the hierarchical organization of data. Different types of file systems include disc files, database files, transaction files, network files, and special files like procfs in UNIX information about processes running on the computer.

A typical data storage device consists of fixed size arrays, blocks, or sectors of 512 bytes each. They consist of a hierarchical (that is, with directories) or flat file system. Computer files are generally stored using storage devices, hard discs, or CD-ROMs.

9.1.5 Multimedia Files

Because of the presence of streaming data like audio or video, multimedia files introduce additional challenges. One such challenge is that different media types need to be displayed continuously; that is, data need to be played in real time. The second challenge is to synchronize pictures with audio. The third difference compared to discrete data files (traditional) is the file size. Audio and video need much more storage space than text does, so the challenge is to organize this data efficiently on a disc within a limited storage space.

9.1.6 Scanners and CCDs

A *scanner* is an optical device that analyzes an image or object and converts it into a digital image. Modern-day scanners are generally desktop or flatbed scanners, although older handheld scanners are sometimes used. A CCD or contact image sensor (CIS) is used as an image sensor. Older versions used photomultiplier tubes. Different types include planetary scanners for photographing books and objects, three-dimensional (3D) scanners for 3D objects, and digital cameras that use reprographic cameras.

A CCD, also known as a color-capture device, is an image sensor consisting of an integrated circuit and an array of coupled or linked light sensitive capacitors. It is used in digital photography, astronomy (photometry), medical fluoroscopy, ultraviolet (UV) spectroscopy, and so on.

9.1.7 Solid State and Flash Drives

These drives are essentially discs that do not have moving parts. Flash is the implementation that enables this process. USB flash drives and secure digital (SD) cards are examples. USB thumb drives use flash storage.

9.1.8 Cloud Storage

Cloud storage is a model of computer data storage where digital data is stored in logical pools. The physical storage is embodied in multiple servers and even multiple locations. The physical storage is generally owned and managed by hosting companies. Methods of access are:

1. Co-located cloud computing services
2. Web service application programming interfaces (APIs) like cloud desktop storages, cloud storage gateways, or Web-based content management systems.

Usability is a great advantage provided a copy of the file to be stored is saved on the desktop. Although bandwidth availability is, in principle, an advantage, companies usually provide limited bandwidth; for extra bandwidth, the extra charge is quite appreciable. Internet access is required for accessibility. Disaster recovery is possible, but data is not always secure. Cost saving and memory saving are also advantages. However, when manipulating files locally through multiple devices, the services to be operated on the files need to be downloaded on all the devices used. A cloud computing model is shown in Figure 9.1.

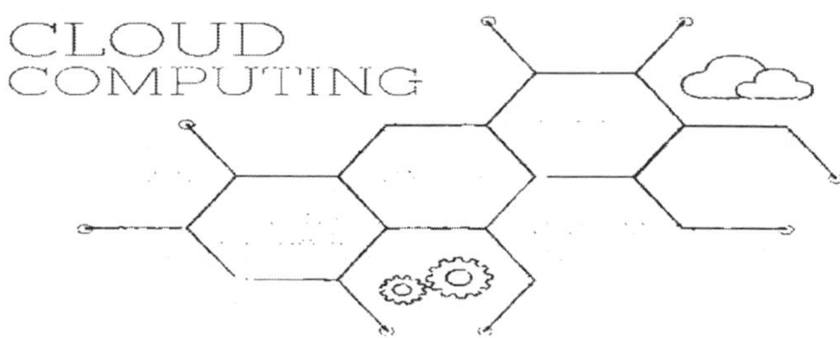

FIGURE 9.1
Cloud computing model. (Created by Rawpixel.com-Freepik.com.)

9.2 Multimedia Data Management Systems

A multimedia data management system (MMDBMS) manages different types of data in different types of formats for a wide array of media. Mainly four different types of data need to be managed: text, image, audio, and video. Among these, text is the easiest to manage because it can be indexed, ordered, and searched using string management techniques. Simple sounds can be managed by representing audio as a sequence of signals over different channels. Image and video database management is a challenging task that has received much attention over recent years. Techniques applied to images can be extended to video.

9.2.1 Image Processing

For image management, several image-processing techniques have been used: image enhancement, representation, and segmentation [7].

Image enhancement: The aim of image enhancement is to improve the interpretability or perception of information in images for human viewers, or to provide input for other automated image-processing techniques that is an improvement over the original image. The two broad categories of image enhancement are:

1. Spatial domain methods: These methods operate directly on pixels.
2. Frequency domain methods: These operate on the Fourier transform of an image.

There is no hard-and-fast rule for determining what is good image enhancement when it comes to human perception. When image enhancement techniques are used as pre-processing tools for other image processing techniques, then quantitative measures can determine which techniques are most suitable for the application at hand.

Image representation: Quantized images are commonly represented as sets of pixels encoding color and brightness information in a matrix. An alternative method is based on contour line. A contour representation is useful for easy retrieval of the full image in bitmap form and is used primarily for data compression of an image. The principle is to encode, at each level, the boundaries of connected regions of pixels at levels greater than or equal to a preselected value. It is easy to reconstruct an original image from these boundaries. Output-sensitive algorithms are available for computing contour representation.

Image segmentation: Segmentation distinguishes objects of interest from the background. For intensity images (that is, those represented by point-wise intensity levels), four popular approaches are threshold techniques, edge-based methods, region-based techniques, and connectivity-preserving relaxation methods, discussed in Chapter 4.

Threshold techniques utilize local pixel information for decision making. These techniques are effective when the intensity levels of the objects fall squarely outside the range of levels in the background because spatial information is ignored. However, blurred region boundaries are undesirable.

Edge-based methods center around contour detection. Since these methods are not able to connect broken contour lines, they are prone to failure in the presence of blurring.

A *region-based method* partitions the image into connected regions by grouping neighboring pixels of similar intensity levels. Some criterion involving homogeneity or sharpness of region boundaries is used to merge adjacent regions. Problems with region-based methods include fragmentation caused by overly stringent criteria or blurred boundaries caused by lenient ones and resulting in overmerging. Hybrid techniques using a mix of the above-mentioned methods are also popular.

Texture segmentation: Texture is a local variation in an image. Even images with the same overall intensity can look quite different. To segment texture, the following steps are adopted: Characterize the local texture first. Then compute statistics like a histogram, averages, standard deviations, to name a few.

Motion segmentation for video is useful when there is a sequence of images of a scene. Motion detection then becomes a useful way of finding objects. The essential steps are:

1. Take two or more consecutive images of a scene.
2. Then look for differences between these images to detect motion.
3. Finally, group moving areas into objects.

A connectivity-preserving relaxation-based segmentation method, usually referred to as the active contour model (ACM), is also a popular segmentation scheme. The main idea is to start with some initial boundary shape represented in the form of spline curves and then iteratively modify it by applying various shrink and expansion operations according to some predefined energy function.

9.2.2 Content-Based Image Retrieval

Content-based image retrieval (CBIR) is a recently developed methodology [8] that indexes and retrieves images based on their visual content. The visual features can be classified as general features, which include color, shape, and texture, and domain-specific features, for example, objects within the image.

CBIR is used in the management of image archives, art galleries and museums, World Wide Web (WWW) image indexing, science databases (e.g., medicine, astronomy, geography), industry-specific uses, trademark databases, textiles and fabrics advertising, architecture, and design.

The basic content of images can be identified with the help of low-level features like color, shape, texture, and compactness, to name a few. Color within an image is one of the most popular defining features and can be determined by means of a color histogram. The histogram can be divided into groups, and the percentage of each group is measured. A distance metric is used to ascertain the similarity for each color group.

Texture can be described by using several types of features, for example, smoothness, periodicity, directionality, and so on. Region size is matched with image characteristics, which are computed using filter banks, for instance, Gabor wavelets. The weighted vector space matching is performed and is usually used in combination with a color histogram.

Shape can be identified with turning angle, moments of inertia, and pattern spectrum. These features within an image can be represented using feature vectors. Compactness is the ratio of the area to the square of the perimeter.

Images can be represented using a set of feature vectors, with each component of the feature vector corresponding to a feature, for instance, shape, color, and so on. The query should be represented by the same set of feature vectors. Appropriate similarity functions are then selected for the matching procedure. The similarity function should be a good approximation of the human perception of similarity between the prototype and the query images.

9.2.3 Searching

Similarity search [9] is the process of locating a record in a database that is closest to the query. Similarity searching is performed using nearest neighbor finding. Existing methods fall into two classes:

1. A mapping to a low dimension vector space, a process known as dimensionality reduction, is performed. This is then indexed using representations such as quad trees, kD trees, and R-trees.
2. Mapping and indexing of objects is based on distances using representations such as VP tree and Mtree.

9.2.4 Indexing

Indexing is used to prune the search [9]. Some criteria used in indexing schemes include the determination order of magnitude of difference between I/O and CPU cost, the ability to upscale the data, and the ability to incorporate the increase of the data, and also be able to accommodate the complexity of the data and search.

The different indexing schemes are listed below:

1. Memory type algorithms are main memory algorithms like quadtrees and kD trees, or secondary storage algorithms like R-trees and VA files.
2. The access methods could be:
    a. Primary key access, where the query attribute is unique. Examples include hashing and B-trees.
    b. Secondary key access like inverted files; kD tree is an example.
    c. Spatial access like R-trees and space filling curves.
3. The indexing scheme can be data or hypothesis driven. Data-driven approaches are bottom-up approaches where the index is built on existing data and the search is conducted in this fixed data structure. Hypothesis-driven approaches are top-down approaches where the query is characterized and data with similar characteristics are returned.
4. An indexing scheme can be model space or feature space. The coordinate system of the model is referred to as model space. The feature space is the space spanned by the different features used to characterize the data.
5. Search and indexing is based on nearest neighbor or range search. Nearest neighbors like k nearest neighbors are the (k) closest neighbors in feature space. Range search is the pre-processing of a set of objects to determine which of the objects of this set intersect with the query object defined within a range.
6. The partitioning or mapping approach can be data partitioning or space partitioning as well as mapping. Examples of each approach are listed below.

    1. R-tree, SS-tree, kD tree with median split are examples of data partitioning.
    2. Quadtree and kd-tree with fixed split are examples of space partitioning.
    3. Mapping can be implemented using space-filling curves and multidimensional scaling.

9.2.5 Quadtree Algorithms

The space is split into 2k equal sub-squares, k being the number of dimensions. This process is continued until there is only one pixel or point left. It is also possible to split one dimension at a time. kD trees are another variant of this technique. In a nearest neighbor algorithm, the initial range r is regarded as ∞. In a range search, only the nodes within a finite radius r is investigated.

9.2.6 kD Trees

An example of a multidimensional binary search tree is the kD tree. Each node of the tree has two pointers. The node itself holds a record. The pointers can either be null pointers or pointers to another node. The tree is arranged in hierarchical levels, with each level dealing with an attribute. Partitioning of this n-dimensional space with respect to the attributes alternates between the various attributes of this space.

In this method, only one-dimensional splits are allowed. Instead of splitting in the middle, the split should be carefully chosen. The advantages are no (or less) empty spaces, and the space is only linear space. The query time is at most O *(n1−1/k+m)* with *m* number of NNs. This method is ineffective when the dimension of the space is greater than 20. It may be noted here that, the kD tree is a top-down approach.

9.2.7 R Trees

R trees are bottom-up approaches where one starts a with a set of points or rectangles and partitions the set into groups of small cardinalities. For each group, the minimum rectangle containing objects from this group is identified.

The advantages of an R-tree search scheme include the use of the nearest neighbor search scheme, and the scheme works for points and rectangles. Empty spaces are avoided. There are many variants of this scheme, for example, the X tree, SS tree, and SR tree, to mention a few.

Like the kD tree, this method is not effective for multidimensional space.

Review

At the end of this chapter you will have learned about the following topics:

- Magnetic, optical, SSD, and cloud storage media, and their advantages and disadvantages.
- Scanners and CCDs and their functionality.
- CBIR.
- Search and indexing of multimedia content in multimedia databases.

Review Questions

1. How does magnetic media store images and what are its advantages and disadvantages?
2. What is optical media and what are its advantages and disadvantages?
3. Give examples, with explanations wherever needed, of magnetic and optical media.
4. What are scanners and CCDs used for?
5. What is CBIR?
6. How is multimedia search and indexing carried out?
7. Describe the quadtree, kD tree, and R tree search techniques.

Multiple-Choice Questions

1. Magnetic discs are subdivided into:
   (a) Track, region, sector
   (b) Track, region, cylinder
   (c) Track, region, sector, cylinder
   (d) None of the above
2. Which of the following is NOT a magnetic media?
   (a) IDE
   (b) SCSI
   (c) CD-ROM
   (d) RAID
3. Which of the following is NOT an advantage of multimedia?
   (a) Low cost
   (b) High speed
   (c) Removable media
   (d) Random access capability
4. Which of the following are image segmentation techniques?
   (a) Edge-based and region-based techniques
   (b) Connectivity preserving relaxation techniques and thresholding
   (c) Both a and b
   (d) Neither a nor b

5. Which of the following low-level feature detection techniques is (are) used in CBIR?
   (a) Color
   (b) Shape
   (c) Texture
   (d) All of the above
   (e) None of the above
6. Which of the following search techniques uses mapping to a low-dimension vector space?
   (a) VP tree
   (b) M-tree
   (c) Quadtree
   (d) None of the above
7. Which of the following is (are) characteristic(s) of R trees?
   (a) Bottom-up approach
   (b) Only one-dimensional splits performed
   (c) Works well for multidimensional data
   (d) None of the above

References

1. Ralf Steinmetz, Klara Nahrstedt, *Multimedia: Computing, Communications and Applications*, New Delhi, India: Pearson Education, 1995.
2. Ze-Nian Li and Mark S. Drew, *Fundamentals of Multimedia*, Upper Saddle River, NJ: Pearson Education, 2004.
3. Mrinal K. Mandal, *Multimedia Signals and Systems*, Boston, MA: Kluwer Academic Publishers now part of Springer Science + Business Media, 2003.
4. Prabhat K. Andleigh and Kiran Thakrar, *Multimedia Systems Design*, New Delhi, India: Pearson Education, 1996.
5. Fred Halsall, *Multimedia Communications: Applications, Networks, Protocols and Standards*, New Delhi, India: : Pearson Education, 2001.
6. Kay Vaughan, *Multimedia: Making It Work*, New York: McGraw-Hill, 2004.
7. Robert E. Woods and Rafael C. Gonzalez, *Digital Image Processing*, New York: Prentice Hall Technical Education, 1992.

8. Wengang Zhou, Houqiang Li, and Qi Tian, Recent Advance in Content-based Image Retrieval: A Literature Survey. *arXiv* preprint arXiv:1706.06064, 2017. https://arxiv.org/pdf/1706.06064 (accessed September 2017).
9. Erik Zeitler, Spatial and Multimedia Indexing, 2004, user.it.uu.se/~zeitler/seminars/spmm20041201.ppt Erik Zeitler UDBL, Uppsala University, Sweden, (accessed January 2004).

Further Reading

1. user.it.uu.se/~zeitler/seminars/spmm20041201.ppt Erik Zeitler UDBL.
2. cs.wustl.edu/~pless/.../11.w.html/f11_3w.gif.

10

Multimedia Communication and Networking Issues

10.1 Computer and Multimedia Networks: Hardware and Software Issues

Computer networks are essential for computer communications. Multimedia networks have many similarities with computer networks [1,2], including include network layers, multiplexing technologies, LAN and WAN, and peripheral interfaces. Some of the overlapping issues are discussed in the following sections. Multimedia networking systems are based on layers, protocols, and services. A service is a set of operations for requesting applications. A group of logically related services forms layers according to the open systems interconnection (OSI) model. Each layer constitutes a service provide to the preceding layer above. The services describe the behavior of the layer as well as its constituent service elements, known as service data units (SDUs). A protocol is a set of rules to be followed by peer layer instances when two peers communicate. The protocol consists of two parts: the format (or syntax) and the meaning (or semantics) of the exchanged data units, known as peer data units (PDUs). Peer instances are communicated cooperatively between different computers for providing services. In multimedia communications, the application places its requirements on the services and protocols.

10.1.1 Network Layers

Network communication is a complex task and thus involves multiple layers of protocols [1,2]. One such multilayer protocol architecture is the OSI protocol proposed by the International Organization for Standardization (ISO) in 1984. The OSI network model has seven layers, as depicted in Table 10.1.

However, the transmission control protocol/Internet protocol (TCP/IP) is a more practical protocol than OSI. This protocol has five layers (Table 10.1) and has gained wider acceptance. It is connection-oriented and provides reliable data transfer between pairs of communicating processes across the network. TCP relies on IP to deliver the message to the destination computer specified

TABLE 10.1

Multimedia Protocol Stack Compared with OSI and TCP/IP

OSI	TCP/IP	Multimedia
Application layer	Application layer	Application layer
Presentation layer		Multimedia integral control and synchronization layer
Session layer		
Transport layer	Transport layer	Interprocess communication and synchronization layer
Network layer	Network layer	Network layer
Data link layer	Data link layer	
Physical layer	Physical layer	

by its IP address. TCP is slow, however, and in many real-time multimedia applications such as streaming video and voice over IP (VOIP), speed of transmission is the most important criterion. In such cases, the user datagram protocol (UDP), a connectionless protocol is used. A comparison of the multimedia protocol stack with OSI layers and a TCP/IP stack is given in Table 10.1.

10.1.2 Multiplexing Technologies

Modern computer communication links require high capacity. When the link capacity greatly exceeds any individual user's data rate, multiplexing is used to enable users to share the capacity. Some of the basic multiplexing technologies [1,2] include frequency division multiplexing (FDM), where multiple channels are arranged according to their frequency and used for analog data; time division multiplexing (TDM), which is useful for directly multiplexing digital data; and wavelength division multiplexing (WDM), which is used for data transmission through optical fibers. Some modern technologies like integrated services digital network (ISDN) use duplex channels for data transmission using synchronous TDM; synchronous optical NETwork (SONET), in which electrical signals are converted to optical signals before transmission and reconverted after their reception and uses synchronous TDM; and asymmetric digital subscriber line (ASDL), which uses FDM to multiplex three channels.

10.1.3 Network Issues and Topologies

Multimedia communication requires numerous nodes for connecting different applications and devices. Computer communication networks for multimedia can be classified according the extent of the geographical area that they cover and the arrangement of their topology.

10.1.3.1 Topologies

Physical topologies or the physical layouts of nodes in a network can occur in three basic shapes: bus, ring, and star. Hybrid setups are also possible.

Bus topologies: Bus topologies consist of a single cable called the bus that connects all network nodes without intervening connectivity devices. These devices share responsibility for getting data from one point to another. Terminators stop signals when they reach the end of wire. Signal bounce is prevented.

Advantages: Inexpensive, easy to add to, suitable for small networks.

Disadvantages: It is difficult to troubleshoot. It is not fault-tolerant and not very scalable, has high management costs, and the potential for network traffic congestion exists.

Ring topologies: In a ring topology, each node is connected to the two nearest nodes, so the entire network forms a circle.

Advantages: It is reliable and easier to manage as defective node or cable problems are easier to locate. High volumes of network traffic can be handled. Transmission of signals over long distances is possible.

Disadvantages: It is expensive because it requires more network and cable equipment. There is less room for expansion to high-speed communications and thus it is less popular than bus topologies.

Star topologies: In star topologies, every node on the network is connected through a central device, with any single cable connecting only two devices. This reduces cable problems to only two devices. Since more cable is required than is needed for ring and bus networks, this topology is fault-tolerant. It can be easily moved, isolated, or interconnected with other networks and is thus scalable. It can supports a maximum of 1024 addressable nodes on logical network topologies.

Advantages: This is the most popular and easiest to use topology in modern networks because of its ease of management, low start-up costs, scope for expansion, and availability of equipment.

Disadvantages: The single hub is a point of failure and requires more cable than bus.

Logical topologies: A logical topology defines how data can be transmitted between nodes. This might not be like the physical topologies, although similar shapes like bus or ring are possible.

10.1.3.2 LAN and WAN

A local area network (LAN) is confined to a small geographical area and generally uses the broadcast technique. The common types of LANs are as follows:

Ethernet: An ethernet is a packet-switched bus network, although a star LAN network is also possible. The maximum data rate for an ethernet is 10 Mbps, although fast ethernet with a data rate of 100 Mbps is possible.

Token ring: As the name suggests, stations in the token ring are connected by the ring topology. Data rates of the token ring are 4 or 16 Mbps.

Fiber-distributed data interface (FDDI): The FDDI is a successor of the token ring. It has a dual ring topology. The primary ring is used for data transmission; the secondary ring is for fault tolerance. If damage is detected on both rings, they are joined together to function as a single ring. The typical bit rate for FDDI is 100 Mbps.

Wide area network (WAN): A WAN covers a large geographical area encompassing cities and countries. This network uses switching technologies instead of broadcast. Two switching technologies are used: circuit switching and packet switching. The later variants of packet switching are frame relay and cell relay. Circuit switching has a fixed data rate; packet switching allows a variable data rate.

In *circuit switching*, end-to-end circuits need to be made and dedicated for the duration of the connection at a guaranteed bandwidth. To cater to multiple users and variable data rates, FDM or synchronous TDM multiplexing is used. This type of switching is inefficient for multimedia communication.

In *packet switching*, data is broken into small packets of 1000 bytes or less before transmission. The header of each packet contains control information like destination address, routine, and so on.

Frame relay is a cheaper version of packet switching with minimal services. It usually has frame lengths up to 1600 bytes.

Cell relay uses small and fixed length (53 bytes) packets called cells. This is used in the *asynchronous transfer mode (ATM)*, and so ATM is sometimes referred to as cell relay. ATM used 53 bytes per packet, with five bytes for the header and 48 bytes for the payload. ATM provides high speed and low delay.

10.1.3.3 Access Network

An access network connects users to the core network and is the last mile for delivering different multimedia services. Examples include Internet access, telephony, and digital and analog TV services.

10.1.3.4 Peripheral Interfaces

The peripheral interfaces connect different peripheral devices like I/O hard discs, printers, CD-ROMs, pointing devices, mice, personal digital assistants (PDAs), digital cameras, webcams, and so on.

10.1.4 Internet Protocols

Some of the protocols involved in providing multimedia over the Internet are outlined below:

IP-multicast: A broadcast message is sent to all nodes in the domain, a unicast message is sent to only one node, and a multicast message is sent to a set of specified nodes. IP-multicast enables multicast on the Internet. Its uses include mailing lists, group file transfer, audio/video on demand, and audio/video conferencing. The Internet Multicast Backbone (MBone) is used for audio/video conferencing. MBone uses a subnetwork of routers (m-routers, also known as islands) that support multicast to forward multicast packets, which are encapsulated inside regular IP packets for tunneling to the destination via these islands. The Internet Group Management Protocol (IGMP) is used for the management of multicast groups.

Real-time transport protocol (RTP): This protocol was an improvement over the original protocol, designed for the transport of real-time data like audio and video streaming and audio/video conferencing. Although intended for multicast, it can also be used for unicasting.

Real-time control protocol (RTCP): RTCP is a companion of RTP, used to monitor quality of service (QoS) regarding quality of data transmission, audio/video conferencing, information about participants, and so on.

Resource reservation protocol (RSVP): RSVP is a setup protocol for Internet resource reservation. This protocol is used to guarantee the desirable QoS for multicast as well as unicast.

Real-time streaming protocol (RTSP): Earlier multimedia data was transmitted over the large network file. More recently, audio and video data is transmitted from a stored media server to the client in a data stream that is instantly decoded as streaming audio/video. RTSP is a protocol for communication between a client and a stored media server.

Internet telephony: Internet telephony is not restricted to VoIP but can be integrated into voice, video, and data services. It is supported by RTP with control protocol RTCP. For streaming media, RTSP is used; RSVP takes care of Internet resource reservation. The **session initiation protocol (SIP)** is an application layer control protocol used to establish as well as terminate Internet telephony sessions. It and can be used for VoIP as well as multimedia conferences and multimedia distribution.

10.1.5 Multimedia over ATM

ATM is a high-speed network with little delay, making it a modern-day choice for multimedia communication. In addition, the advent of the video coding standard H.264 has facilitated the use of multimedia over ATM for high data generating multimedia applications like video-on-demand and real-time telephony. Four classes of service exist in ATM. The class of service to be used depends on the required bit rate for the multimedia application for which it is used. The advantages of multimedia over ATM are:

1. The three different kinds of data (data, video, and voice) can be merged into a single network.
2. ATM is a standard that allows different bandwidth and QoS guarantees.

10.2 QoS and Synchronization Issues

In Internet networks, QoS is an industry-based standard in which transmission rates, error rates, and other parameters can be measured and improved in advance. In the following, the factors affecting QoS are discussed. In multimedia, alignment of entities with respect to content, spatial layout, and time (for temporal data like audio and video) is referred to as synchronization.

10.2.1 QoS

Multimedia data involves continuous data, which introduces additional complications in network transmission for the following reasons:

1. Large volumes of data.
2. This data is real-time and interactive, so low delay and synchronization between audio and video are required.
3. With the fluctuation of data rates, there can be long phases of no transmission and bursts to high volume data.

These considerations prompt the need for examining the QoS for multimedia data communication. The parameters which determine QoS are as follows:

1. *Data rate* is the measure of the transmission speed in kilobits per sec, or megabits per sec.
2. *Latency* is the maximum frame or packet delay. This indicates the maximum time needed from transmission to reception and is measured in milliseconds (ms). If the round-trip delay exceeds 50 ms in voice communication, then echo becomes perceptible; when the one-way delay is longer than 250 ms, talker overlap occurs.
3. *Packet loss* or *error* gives the percentage error of the packet data transmission.
4. *Jitter* or *delay jitter* is a measure of the smoothness of the audio/video playback. Jitter is related to the variance of frame/packet delays.
5. *Sync skew* is a measure of the multimedia data synchronization, in ms. For accurate lip synchronization, the limit of sync skew is ±80 ms between audio and video. The general acceptable value is ±200 ms.

10.2.2 Types of Synchronization

Synchronization in multimedia systems includes content and spatial and temporal relations between media objects. Content relation defines the dependency of media objects for some data. An example is the spreadsheet and the graphics that represent the data given in the spreadsheet. Spatial relation defines the spatial layout for the presentation of media objects on an output device at a certain point of the media presentation. An example is desktop publishing. Temporal relation defines time dependencies between media objects. Lip synchronization is an example.

Temporal objects are streaming objects like audio and video. Non-temporal objects are objects like text and images.

10.2.3 Temporal Synchronization

Temporal synchronization involves relations between temporal and non-temporal media objects, which can be of two types:

1. *Intra-object synchronization*: Time relation between various presentation units of one time-dependent media object, for example, time relation between single frames of video.
2. *Inter-object synchronization*: synchronization between media objects, for example, audio/video sequence followed by animation.

Synchronization can occur at several levels, for example, the operating system or lower communication level layers or during the middleware/session layer or during the application layer. The latter two occur during runtime.

During presentation, the temporal relations, as they existed during the capturing process, can be reproduced for live synchronization. In synthetic synchronization, temporal relations are artificially specified; that is, stored data objects provide new combined multimedia objects via artificial temporal relations. There are two phases of temporal relations: the specification phase, which defines the temporal relations, and the presentation phase, which presents data in the sync mode.

Time-dependent media objects consist of time-dependent presentation units known as logical data units (LDUs).

10.2.4 Synchronization Accuracy Specification Factors

Synchronization accuracy specification factors are used to specify the goodness of a sync. They include the following:

1. *Delay*: Delay specifies the end-to-end delay and gives a measure of the time difference between transmission and reception. For audio, the one-way delay should be between 100 and 500 msec. For high-definition television (HDTV), this delay should be less than 50; for broadcast analog television, it should be less than 100 ms for broadcast. For video conferencing, it should be less than 500 msec.
2. *Delay jitter*: Delay jitter indicates the instantaneous difference between the desired presentation times and the actual presentation times of streamed multimedia data. This should be 10 times better than delay.
3. *Skew*: Skew gives the average difference between the desired presentation time and the actual presentation time.
4. *Error rate*: The error rate is the level of error specified by the bit error rate (BER). BER ranges from.01 for telephones to .000001 for HDTV.

Review

At the end of this chapter you will have learned about the following topics:

Network layers

Multiplexing technologies

Network topologies

Access networks

LAN and WAN and peripheral interfaces

Different Internet protocols: IP-multicast, RTP, RTCP, RSVP, real-time streaming, Internet telephony

Multimedia over ATM

Quality of service and synchronization

Review Questions

1. What are the different network layers in OSI, TCP/IP, and multimedia?
2. What are the different multiplexing technologies?
3. Describe the different network topologies.
4. Describe briefly LAN and WAN.
5. List the different Internet protocols and state their salient features.
6. Which parameters determine the QoS?
7. What are the different types of synchronization?
8. Write a brief paragraph about temporal synchronization.
9. What are the synchronization accuracy specification factors?

Multiple-Choice Questions

1. Which of the following is a (are) TCP/IP network layer(s)?
   (a) Application layer
   (b) Data layer
   (c) Network layer
   (d) All of the above
2. Which of the following are network topologies?
   (a) Bus, ring, star, logical
   (b) Bus, ring, star
   (c) Logical, star
   (d) Bus, ring

3. ISDN uses which of the following multiplexing technologies?
   (a) FDM
   (b) TDM
   (c) WDM
   (d) None of the above
4. The typical bit rate for FDDI is:
   (a) 4 Mbps
   (b) 10 Mbps
   (c) 16 Mbps
   (d) 100 Mbps
5. Which of the following protocols monitor QoS regarding quality of data transmission, audio/video conferencing, and information about participants?
   (a) RTP
   (b) RTCP
   (c) RSVP
   (d) IGMP
6. Which of the following parameters affect quality of service?
   (a) Latency
   (b) Sync Skew
   (c) Jitter
   (d) All of the above
7. Which of the following is not a type of synchronization?
   (a) Content relation
   (b) Spatial relation
   (c) Temporal relation
   (d) Temperature relation

References

1. Ralf Steinmetz and Klara Nahrstedt, *Multimedia: Computing, Communications and Applications*, New Delhi, India: Pearson Education, 1995.
2. Ze-Nian Li and Mark S. Drew, *Fundamentals of multimedia*, New Delhi, India: Pearson, Prentice-Hall, 2004.

Appendix: Solutions

Chapter 1

MCQ

1. (c) 2. (e) 3. (d) 4. (e) 5. (e) 6. (d) 7. (d) 8. (e) 9. (c) 10. (e).

Chapter 2

MCQ

1. (d) 2. (d) 3. (c) 4. (d) 5. (d) 6. (e) 7. (e) 8. (a) 9. (d).

Chapter 3

MCQ

1. (a) 2. (b) 3. (b) 4. (d) 5. (b) 6. (a) 7. (e) 8. (a, b) 9. (e) 10. (d).

Chapter 4

MCQ

1. (c) 2. (a) 3. (b) 4. (d) 5. (c) 6. (c) 7. (d) 8. (b) 9. (c) 10. (a).

Chapter 5

MCQ

1. (c) 2. (d) 3. (a) 4. (c) 5. (a) 6. (b) 7. (b) 8. (c) 9. (b) 10. (b).

Chapter 6

MCQ

1. (a) 2. (c) 3. (a) 4. (c) 5. (e) 6. (e) 7. (d) 8. (d) 9. (e) 10. (d).

Chapter 7

MCQ

1. (b) 2. (a) 3. (a) 4. (c).

Chapter 8

MCQ

1. (c) 2. (b) 3. (d) 4. (d) 5. (d) 6. (e) 7. (a)-false (b)-true (c)-false 8. (a) anchor; (b) Pointers link two nodes of a graph 9. (d)

Chapter 9

MCQ

1. (a) 2. (c) 3. (a) 4. (c) 5. (c) 6. (a) 7. (a).

Chapter 10

MCQ

1. (d) 2. (a) 3. (b) 4. (d) 5. (b) 6. (d) 7. (d).

Index

Note: Page numbers in italic and bold refer to figures and tables, respectively.